BRIGHT TRACKS

BRIGHT TRACKS
To Greece by rail in 1959

RICHARD PIKE

*With many contemporary photographs
by the author and Christopher Elston*

Copyright © 2017 Richard Pike

The moral right of the author has been asserted.

Apart from any fair dealing for the purposes of research or private study, or criticism or review, as permitted under the Copyright, Designs and Patents Act 1988, this publication may only be reproduced, stored or transmitted, in any form or by any means, with the prior permission in writing of the publishers, or in the case of reprographic reproduction in accordance with the terms of licences issued by the Copyright Licensing Agency. Enquiries concerning reproduction outside those terms should be sent to the publishers.

Matador
9 Priory Business Park,
Wistow Road, Kibworth Beauchamp,
Leicestershire. LE8 0RX
Tel: 0116 279 2299
Email: books@troubador.co.uk
Web: www.troubador.co.uk/matador
Twitter: @matadorbooks

ISBN 978 1785898 662

British Library Cataloguing in Publication Data.
A catalogue record for this book is available from the British Library.

Printed and bound by CPI Group (UK) Ltd, Croydon, CR0 4YY
Typeset in 12pt Aldine401 BT by Troubador Publishing Ltd, Leicester, UK

Matador is an imprint of Troubador Publishing Ltd

In memory of Rev Canon John B Bayley

…there are bright tracks
Where I have been,
And there grow flowers
For others' delight.
Think well, O singer,
Soon comes night.

Ivor Gurney

ACKNOWLEDGEMENTS

The dedicatory quotation from the Ivor Gurney poem "The Songs I Had" and the title itself are reproduced here with kind permission of the Ivor Gurney Estate.

I owe an enormous debt of gratitude to my cousin, David Pike, for the care he took and the time he devoted to enhancing my fifty-year-old colour pictures which had been suffering badly from the dust of time and the sand of Greece.

I would also like to thank Tim Wilson for his help and encouragement with this project and my many friends at Ancaster, Leicester and Peterborough who have heard me read extracts from this account and have suggested improvements to the text. Thank you for your support.

The majority of the photographs in this book are contemporary and taken either by Chris Elston or myself. A few, however, have been found online, which I have gratefully used. Detailed acknowledgements of those pictures are given at the end.

Finally, I am lucky to be able to include cartoons and sketches done by John Bayley and to reproduce, with thanks, some sketches done by Mike Stewardson at the time.

Any errors of fact or memory are mine entirely.

TO THE READER

I always knew I'd one day write this account of the longest and most memorable holiday all of us ever had. But it has taken a very long time to bring it to the printed page. I have called it a *re-creation* of our time in Greece. By that I mean that I have attempted to bring to life again how it was for us all more than fifty-five years ago. But it is not entirely a fictional piece. The primary source for these accounts is notes I made at the time in a screwed-up school exercise book stuffed into my rucksack, trying where possible to capture significant moments with little one-word memory joggers or longer notes. Some of them have become meaningless over time, though they were important enough as we experienced them.

Conversations are largely fictional, though some things were actually said and have stuck in my memory. I also have tried to bring out something of my friends' characters in what they say and talk about.

As well as my notes, I was able to draw on letters and postcards I sent back home which were carefully saved for me by my mother and my girlfriend at the time. I'm fortunate also to be able to refer to correspondence Chris sent home, also carefully preserved. I've been grateful for photocopies of that and other documents he retained.

Chris is also responsible for the excellent black and white photographs which illustrate our travels. Most of the colour pictures are my own, taken as colour slides. Other pictures have been culled from elsewhere and acknowledgements for them are made at the end.

★ ★ ★

A Word of Warning

In some ways this is a slice of social history or like opening a time capsule. It does contain specific language which we used at the time but which would now be regarded as unacceptable and inappropriate. So, too, we show certain attitudes of prejudice and arrogance. Since the time of our trip, we have all grown up and changed, as has society. None of us would subscribe to or endorse those attitudes now.

But we did then…

The Land Where Nay Means Yes

In the summer of 1959, the year in which most of our group were twenty-one, when Harold Macmillan was Prime Minister, and we'd never had it so good, a small group from King's set out for a travelling holiday during the long vacation which took just over five weeks. It was probably the last time before retirement we'd ever enjoy so much free time.

Most of us were reading Classics at Cambridge; one of our party, Mike, was not; he was a medic but keenly interested in the Arts. I doubt the idea of such an adventure would have occurred to us had the College not been generous and given some of us travel grants.

We'd always been modest about belonging to a college that was considered wealthy after skilful investment earlier in the century, probably by Maynard Keynes: King's seemed to make the most of its money. I don't suppose any of us appreciated the liberal attitude of the college using its money to encourage its undergraduates to travel. We were pretty insular; certainly many of us needed something to broaden our minds.

My travel grant of £40 was a substantial sum. At that time, a gallon of Esso Golden – the top grade petrol – was five shillings (25p) and a pint of beer less than 10p. We felt we had to spend the grant on something memorable. We decided we'd go to Greece.

To us it seemed as distant as the moon, but, since we were studying its ancient culture and history, it was an interesting and obvious destination. Travel to Greece was unusual then – a mere fourteen years after the war. The country seemed a long way away and scarcely ready for tourism. In many ways we expected things to be rather primitive. Flying there wasn't even considered. We'd travel the whole way by train – a three-day journey from London Victoria to Athens, on The Tauern Express. The fare was £22 return, quite expensive, we felt then. We were to be part of a larger group organised by an undergraduate entrepreneur, Brian Hughes. And when we got to Greece, we'd sleep outside under the stars, except in Athens, where a cheap hotel was booked for our first few nights.

Medical preparations were elaborate; we needed the combined TABT jab against typhoid and paratyphoid which was also anti-tetanus. We also had to have a certificate proving we'd been vaccinated, in order to avoid the danger of smallpox. Most children were vaccinated as routine while still very young. I wasn't, because my father objected, believing the procedure unsafe. He claimed that two of his siblings died in rural Lincolnshire in the early part of the 20th century as a result of vaccination.

Since I'd not been vaccinated, I had to have a sore *left* arm as well as my right one. Interesting to watch the pox-scab develop. It looked like a scarab beetle clinging to your upper arm and stayed for about two weeks. Because the limb was likely to be stiff and painful in the early stages, it was better to choose the left arm if you were right-handed, and, to avoid any complications, you had to be particularly careful not to knock the scab before it was ready to drop off by itself. It left an ugly oval scar. Girls, to avoid this slight disfigurement, and to leave their upper arm smooth and attractive, often had the vaccination on the thigh where the pock-mark was supposed to be less visible.

Because of the extreme heat in Greece, we were advised to take salt tablets with us and swallow them regularly on our travels round the country in order to replace salt lost through sweating. No one warned us against dehydration, and the ubiquitous plastic water-bottles of today were not available: we took metal water flasks, if we had them, off our sports bikes. Water purification tablets, insect repellent and ant powder were also regarded as essential. No one told us to protect ourselves against the sun, though we were advised to buy a cheap hat when we got there. In those days, wisdom had it that you should cover yourself in olive oil if you wanted a really good tan. On the whole, our preparations were more for the tropics than the Eastern Mediterranean.

Backpacking, then, and outdoor camping. We wouldn't require a tent because rain was unlikely – there'd be nothing between us and the open sky. We needed to travel light: a few changes of clothes, a sleeping bag and all our medical stuff. I also packed an inflatable lilo as protection against sleeping directly on the ground. We didn't take guide-books, even if pocket-sized ones existed. Anyway, we knew the sites we wanted to visit. Having sufficient film for our cameras seemed more important. Photographic material would be particularly expensive out there – at least a shilling more per film than in England.

At some point we'd have to decide whether to continue shaving whilst touring around. Wet shaving out of doors might be difficult, and different voltages on the continent made the use of electric razors problematical. The decision was almost made before we left. It'd be interesting to see ourselves with beards for perhaps the only time in our lives.

We believed we'd get by in Greece. We couldn't speak the modern language but at least could read the letters and make sense of some words. We were warned about the contradictory culture where a brief *nod* of the head meant NO, whether it was accompanied by 'οχι (oshee) or not, and where Nay (ναι) meant YES. Above all, we mustn't make the gesture of opening a fist, palm outwards, towards any Greek, since this was highly insulting. Flexing closed fingers to reveal the palm looked a little like throwing dung at someone, but we never discovered why the gesture was offensive or what it symbolised.

We heard travellers' tales, of course, before we left. We'd have to haggle over prices when buying things – definitely not customary for us, brought up in a world of re-sale price maintenance where prices were uniform and fixed. To get a waiter's attention in a bar or restaurant, it was appropriate to clap your hands, they said. We learned to do it, but never felt comfortable with such an imperious gesture.

The Maths don and college aesthete, Norman Routledge, had travelled to Greece in a small party during the long summer vacation the year before.

'How did you get on with the language, Norman?' I asked.

'Oh, weally no bother,' he lisped with characteristic ebullience. 'There were five of us and we just went into a restauwant, and someone said to the waiter something like 'eeny olly olly pendy.'

And he laughed uproariously because it was all Greek to him and sounded just like cheering on a rowing crew.

Life was a gay laugh to Norman.

'What about sunglasses?' I asked.

'What do you want those for? I never bothered. Your pupils are perfectly able to contract in bright light.'

I couldn't fault his logic and from then on I've rarely worn sunglasses, even in strong sunshine.

We went home from Cambridge in early June at the end of our second year, knowing we had six weeks to prepare for our holiday. Not being a hiker or a camper, I needed to borrow a sleeping bag and rucksack. Fascinating how much I could carry when everything was crammed in. I came to appreciate the metal framework which held the sack away from my body and stopped awkward objects poking me in the back. By the standards of modern kit it was small: a mere hump on the back, not a tower above the head like some modern contraptions. Both my lilo and sleeping bag were rolled up and retained by straps at the top.

So, armed with hearsay and travellers' cheques, I prepared for the big expedition.

Financially, the modern traveller to Europe has it easy. You need just one currency wherever you're going and you can rely on credit or debit cards to see you through while you're away. I can still remember viewing hole-in-the-wall cash machines with suspicion when they first appeared in England. Now they are commonplace. But it was a long time before I would go near one. Now you can use them in England or abroad and receive cash in that country's currency. Barclaycard first appeared in 1966 – no such ease of use available to us in 1959.

When we went to Greece, we had to take four different currencies with us. We were advised to take a poundsworth each of Belgian Francs and German Marks – which would probably also be accepted in Austria – a poundsworth of Greek Drachmas to start us off when we arrived in Athens, and £2 in Jugoslav dinars. We needed more cash for Jugoslavia, not because it was more expensive – far from it, but because we would take so long travelling across the country. Nearly twenty-four hours each way. It was the one place where we could get good quality hot food in the restaurant car of the train.

The real bugbear of travelling, probably until the 1980s or later, was having to organise traveller's cheques. They were rarely issued by your own bank. You needed to buy them through the bank from another organisation such as American Express. You had to decide what value each cheque should be so that this could be converted into foreign currency when you got there.

But this itself involved a palaver. One part of the cheque had to be signed before you left England and you signed each of them again in the presence of the paying clerk abroad. You needed to prove your identity at the foreign bank by taking your passport; you had to queue at a particular desk in order to receive your money and had to wait while elaborate calculations were done as to what the correct exchange rate would be. That varied from day to day and place to place. And, finally, the bank also took some of your money as their own commission.

They Shoot You for Less Than That

Thursday 30th July 1959:
I arrived at *Victoria Station* later than the others, clearly carrying more luggage, but pleased to spot familiar faces in the crush that afternoon. Our small group numbered four: Chris Elston, whom I'd known right through school from the age of eleven; Mike Stewardson, my first friend at King's and firm companion, and John Bayley, tall, bespectacled and good-humoured, later to enter the priesthood. We all knew each other well, part of a larger coterie who visited each other in college, listened to music, drank coffee and philosophised the night away.

'Hallo, lad,' said John, as I appeared, 'that's all of us.'

John was a great '*ladder*'.

Strange seeing them outside the Cambridge context, no longer looking like undergraduates. They stood over their rucksacks, animated, jittery, catching up on news. Their excitement was infectious and I quickly joined in their laughter.

The hour for assembling was 2.30 PM. Plenty of time before our Boat Train left; the anxious and the eager had arrived early. A substantial party from the university was to travel to Athens, and once there we'd disperse into smaller groups, going our own way until the return journey. Our unit of four seemed ideal; we could be a group, or pair off, if we wished.

The outgoing party was led by David Soulsby, also from my school but a year ahead of Chris and me. After a preliminary meeting in Cambridge for everybody, marked by his brisk efficiency, we'd nick-named him *The Commander*. As our courier, his job was to ensure we all kept together until we reached Greece.

I looked around, amazed at the noise surrounding me. The platform seemed very crowded. Impossible to tell where our party ended and other student groups began. It must have been a special train, laid on at low cost and offering cheap travel – the equivalent then of a charter flight. Certainly we never got to know all forty-eight members of the Cambridge party, even on the long journey to Athens – thirty male, eighteen female.

The equipment people brought was amusing – a party from Corpus Christi College were dressed in khaki safari kit – clearly ready for the tropics. Difficult to tell whether they were serious; I assumed it was a stunt. No sign of mosquito nets anyway.

'Is *that* your sleeping bag, Mike?'

We eyed a garish bundle of fabric, maroon on one side and light blue with black dots on the other.

'Won't get lost in a crowd,' he rumbled.

'What's that you've got, Pike?' said John. 'A lilo? What do you want that for? Are you soft or something?'

I didn't reply.

The others managed with a rucksack alone, but I clutched a box of foodstuff my mother gave me.

'You can always throw it away when you've finished with it,' she explained

I was glad I had it; we'd planned to live on packed meals for at least 24 hours – even so, I had to put fruit in the top of the rucksack where, needless to say, a banana managed to mash itself over the contents in just one night.

'Quiet please, everybody.'

The chatter subsided.

Not the Commander.

An immaculate figure with a rolled umbrella stood on a station luggage trolley: Brian Hughes, the party organiser. He wished us all a good holiday and asked us to bring back 'tips' about Greece since he planned to write a student travel guide to the country. He could afford to look prosperous – our money paid for his trip to Norway that summer *and* The Commander's passage as our leader.

We edged through the barrier towards the train, quieter now, dwarfed by the occasion and the size of the station. In an urgent crush, we stepped with difficulty around puddles on the platform – the result of heavy rain earlier in the day.

Jostling for space, we clambered aboard the green Southern Region electric train, and peered at each other over our rucksacks which we held on our knees because the overhead luggage racks were already full. Cramped conditions had only just begun.

The journey to Dover seemed annoyingly long. At last the sea and Folkestone; and, within a few minutes, bowed and bent-kneed, our rucksacks like humps on our backs we trudged along the platform of Dover Marine. Beyond the barriers, strict segregation: British and Non-British.

As I filed past the official and showed my passport photograph, he seemed to give me a disbelieving glance. Guilt rushed to my face at such scrutiny. Perhaps he thought I was a smuggler. Obviously a little of my innocence had worn off in the time since my only other trip abroad, six years earlier; I now looked very different from my fifteen year old self.

Le Roi Leopold III was a Belgian boat and appeared already swarming with passengers. We managed to find space on the starboard side for our rucksacks. John even found himself a deckchair below the main deck.

We waited.

A lifeboat slung in the derricks above our heads trickled a stream of water into the scuppers; an apple wormed its way out of the top of my rucksack and rolled playfully out of reach. I was cross. That meant reduced rations.

Still more hanging around before we slipped away from the quay at 5.30pm. Then at last I wedged myself on the ship's railings, pulled out my 35mm Paxette camera, and waited for the right moment to capture our last view of England for five weeks. Time to begin recording our trip.

Most passengers seemed to be students, many in high spirits. Someone began to climb the mast and was ordered down by a sailor. Foreigners returning home seemed quieter, better behaved.

The white cliffs dwindled and faded, and the sky became patched with heavier cloud. Wet weather still threatened. We'd chosen the better side of the boat. A strong wind buffeted the port side and the boat took on a steep list as more and more people crossed over to starboard to take shelter. John was amazed when he left his gust-ridden deckchair and joined us in the comparative calm.

We wandered below into the thick atmosphere of the bar. A chance to get warm; something to pass the time. Chris and Mike decided to buy a bottle of beer each. Expensive by our standards whatever currency they offered, and far too fizzy. Not good old English bitter, at all. Eventually they declared it undrinkable. We weren't yet ready to adapt to Continental beer.

Time dragged; everything had seemed so imminent: we'd even seen the French coast before we left. Nothing to do but wait; we'd not yet learned to take pleasure in the travelling. The crossing wasn't direct and seemed wearisome. Perhaps taking shelter from the strong wind, the boat ploughed North along the coast of France. The grey sea churned and foamed around us.

'We must reach Ostend soon.' I sighed and blew my nose.

Back on deck, we'd lost our places, and had to sit on the exposed bench seats on the port side, bracing ourselves against the cold wind. Time lingered. Darkness and rain threatened. Some German students standing nearby in brief leather shorts looked drawn and bloodless. It became important to ignore the slight roll the ship had taken up, as sea-sickness beckoned.

'As long as I can see the horizon, I'm all right,' Mike said.

We travelled on ships several times during our holiday, often feared a troubled sea and sea-sickness, never did learn why Mike trusted the steadfast gaze into the distance. He said he'd discovered this magic during some nasty experiences on a cramped trawler.

Never found out how he got there, either…

Eventually the engines slowed to a thrum; I'd had enough of the chill air and the long journey, the Channel crossing not the best place for nursing the summer cold I'd brought with me.

July? It felt like March…

The wedge of passengers drove towards the exit. Plenty of time to gaze at the town of *Ostend*: high-storeyed buildings along the front stretched into the darkening distance. The harbour seemed an intruder in a seaside resort. A vast man-made bulwark afforded a passage in and kept the water deep enough for the ferries. I couldn't understand how it worked. We saw beach on both sides – the last holidaymakers packing up, preparing to leave. A few even waved.

In the crush to disembark, our party was scattered. It was some time before I spotted

Mike's familiar sweater and hunched back. That sweater was Mike's trademark; it'd be polite to call its colour *ginger,* but its undertones were subtler, richer in hue and association. It lived with him around Cambridge – easily recognisable when he and other dramatically-inclined undergraduates appeared as extras in the film *Cambridge Blue.* Spot the sweater and you found Mike.

Reassuring, like spying a landmark.

If you couldn't see Mike, you could hear him. His laugh was a distinctive ascending two-tone honk which escaped above any crowd. Anything he found amusing evoked it. He revelled in the absurdities and incompetences of life and, as a lover of *The Goon Show*, often put on funny voices from the programme, like Bluebottle or Henry Crun. Mike was a fund of jokes and silly songs, many of them filthy, as befitted a trainee doctor. He quickly acquired the nickname at college of Doctor Splot.

Because.

Dark in humour and olive-skinned in complexion, he had black floppy hair and soulful dark button eyes set above a shapeless splod of a nose. Like all of us then, he was lean-built and fit.

But watch his long smooth fingers coaxing a Chopin waltz out of a piano or caressing a pencil sketch into life. Listen to him sing or act. I remember quailing before his ability to quote from *Macbeth* which he'd studied at school.

Our relationship was instinctive and instantaneous. Two years previously we both had bed-sits on the first floor landing of a college boarding house in the centre of town, euphemistically called a hostel. Natural to forge a friendship. We looked out for each other in those early days of independent living, quickly fell into the comfortable habit of calling each other 'mate', an unusual term between friends then.

★ ★ ★

After the drab austerity of England, the customs hall at *Ostend* seemed luxurious. A pity we'd nothing to declare; it would have been interesting to linger. We'd marvelled at the marble table tops, fluorescent lighting and the abundance of pot plants. Pressed by others behind, we surged on towards the waiting train. The Commander, efficient as ever, assigned us to our compartment in a very long train made up from different countries' rolling stock. Our coach was Belgian – the only carriage we could be sure was going right through to Athens. Each compartment was meant to take eight people. The four of us found ourselves with Chris Hall and James Wrangham, also from Kings, and two girls from Newnham College: Merle Tong and Janet Newell. All of us, except Mike, reading Classics.

We jostled in, laughing and joking about the accommodation, then slowly we realised this compartment would be home to eight of us and our luggage for the next three days.

'It's impossible,' I said, 'it's narrower than British Railways, and the seats are hard, too.'

Solid, shining, dark green leather, one meagre arm-rest each.

'It's like a cattle truck,' someone said.

'How on earth are we going to sleep in here?' Merle said.

'I'm hungry,' John said, and that changed the subject.

The train moved off at exactly 10 PM, and we all began eating our carefully saved packed supper; most were now very hungry. We all watched Chris Elston as, with careful deliberation, he punctured a tin of beer and poured it into a mug. We envied his foresight; most of us had only water, perhaps squash. John, gangling his legs to get comfortable, somehow knocked the mug off the little window table and the beer spread over the floor. Chris's good mood drained visibly with the beer, but he said nothing; John apologised, and, for the first time that trip, we used the Kleenex tissues someone had brought.

Everything seemed so different and noteworthy. The train sounded smooth and swift – not the rhythmic diddly-dum of home. Someone even suggested it had rubber wheels.

'You know, like the Paris metro.'

More information to digest.

It was raining outside.

Someone in the corridor flung our compartment door open.

'Um, chaps, about sleeping…' The Commander to give us our briefing.

The most efficient way of sleeping eight, he suggested, was to send two people out for a couchette, and then sleep two people head to toe on each of the bench seats, and two on the floor. This seemed impossibly difficult; no one wanted the expense of a couchette.

Chris Hall, who'd done National Service, took control: 'Look, let's put all our rucksacks on the floor and try to make a mound level with the seats…' He had it all thought out; my lilo was commandeered, inflated, and laid over the top of the luggage.

John and I, anxious to keep away from all this organisation, saw no more that night. We wandered up the train and found a smart Austrian or German coach, reassuringly empty, and those compartments were intended to take only six. It was unreserved; we decided we'd stay there for the night.

Trying to make it homely, we drew the curtains and switched off everything except the blue night light. After that, stretched out on a bench seat each, we settled down. John, one of the taller members of the group, with dark hair and large glasses was an easy-going companion – private in many ways. His slow smile revealed large, even teeth and lit up his face. If he could measure his life with food and kip, John was happy. He knew little of what went on that night between 10.45 and 6 AM. Three quarters of an hour after leaving Ostend, John was asleep.

My cold hindered my sleeping, and when the train stopped at various stations, unfamiliar sounds, magnified by the stillness, penetrated my drowsiness. I woke up frequently. Sleeping full-length on a compartment seat was strange: difficult to turn over; only a scrunched up sweater as a pillow; no covering blanket.

I envy those who can sleep on trains: the jolts, the strange silences, the sudden voices -all serve to break the rhythm and the security. I cannot let go. I have to monitor what's going on, ensure everything's on track, explain to myself the various phenomena.

About midnight the compartment door slid open and a cheerful voice announced: 'Bière, Lemonade, Coke.' Not welcome.

The train stopped frequently, then stood throbbing or hissing quietly, settling into the silence. I could hear rain spattering on the roof and dripping onto the windows. It began to drench the curtains and I had to slide the glass closed. A strange environment, strange circumstances to be in. To the men on the platforms our train was a boring job in the early hours; to us it was a home on wheels, moving irrevocably towards Athens. Only louder noises disturbed me now. Once I needed to investigate a strange sound: soldiers whistling in another train. Later, an apologetic customs official looked in, withdrew, assuming we had 'rien à déclarer'.

Somewhere we changed direction.

★ ★ ★

Friday 31st July 1959:
I awoke, cold and cramped, and sneaked a look at my watch: only 5.30 AM. John was still breathing quietly. Our first night of sleeping rough was still luxury in view of what we later experienced. The blinds were down; the compartment grey and comfortless; the wheel-taps smooth, hypnotically regular.

Germany.

Quietly, so as not to wake John, I poked my head round the curtains and sat watching the countryside. Everywhere looked neat and regular, grey in the morning light. Fields of crops or tidy slopes of vines flicking past the window. Amazing to see people cycling along the narrow roads to their employment; others had even started work.

The twisting ribbon of road edged in towards the railway; several lorries and cars queued at level crossings. It could have been winter – the men had heavy raincoats on, the air was cold and damp. Drowsily, John spoke a few words and sat up. I pulled back the curtains and brought day into the compartment. Together, sleepily, we watched the countryside go by. I marvelled at the differences. English people never started so early. Everywhere so organised: clean streets, almost sterile in their tidiness. At home, that very month, the government had introduced a £10 fine for dropping litter. *Keep Britain Tidy*. Clearly the Germans needed no such coercion. We saw pride here, efficiency. Even the farming was done with precision: strips of land, trimly cultivated, stretched away from the railway. Neat vineyards patterned the gentle hillside slopes. From above, I guessed, it would look like the landscape for a model railway.

Still early. No point in joining the others; couldn't be sure they were awake, and nothing to do there except eat, talk, and feel cramped. Why not enjoy the space while we had it? We kept the blinds down on the corridor side to maintain our privacy. Desultory watchers of the day. Slowly the wheel-taps lulled us. I was the first to cradle my head on the little table. We stirred later to the train's firm deceleration; without fuss we pulled into Stuttgart.

It's difficult to judge a city from its railway station. We went through some of Europe's oldest and most famous cities on that journey – Cologne, Munich, Salzburg. Yet our appreciation was limited: a brief glimpse through a cluster of heads at the carriage window, or an anxious stroll up and down a very ordinary platform.

Always the fear of being left behind.

Cambridge had bred us bright but arrogant. Only just adults officially, since the age of majority then was twenty-one, we knew little about life and the world. We were eager to see and learn, perhaps, but also proud to be English and believing in our superiority. Our side won the war. We were happily xenophobic, if not racist. It's appalling now how readily we called foreigners, especially the Greeks, 'Wogs'. Anyone whose language we couldn't speak. No shame; the word was ready parlance amongst us.

Prejudice, too. We saw what we wanted to see. At *Stuttgart*, John and I first spotted our proof that the spirit of Germany hadn't changed. We'd been reared on photographs and war films and saw German arrogance paraded before us. A dazzling hierarchy of railway uniforms.

'Look at those peaked caps. Just like Nazi officers used to wear.'

The high peaked front, giving the wearer added height; the steep slope towards the back of the head; soft, immaculate material.

Through both Germany and Austria, we were struck by the formality, the almost military pride and respect for even minor officials in uniform. Many of the Germans looked fat and self-opinionated; the more pompous they looked, the more important they seemed.

'Look at him strutting! Anyone who still hates the Germans would be annoyed by that,' I said.

'Mm, yes.'

The others were anxious when we rejoined them. Nearly 10 AM now, and the train had been shedding coaches along the route for some time. We walked into a barrage of comments.

'We thought you might have been dropped off.'

'Did you see the Rhine Valley?' James said. 'It was glorious; we saw it just as it was getting light.'

Because we'd kept the blinds down on the corridor side, John and I missed one of the most splendid sights of that journey.

Time for breakfast, I thought. Unfastening the top of my rucksack, I found the banana I'd saved. Just sticky slime on the fabric wall.

Oh, well.

Munich. The first chance to stretch our legs on the platform. It was lower than we expected and seemed a big step down. I puzzled often why the rolling stock and the platforms were not matched in height.

Some people disappeared to find a tap and replace water brought from England. A man with a tray hanging from his neck went by, selling German chocolate. Chris Elston called from a carriage window to buy some. Puzzling out the exchange rate later, we worked out he'd paid something like 2/6 (12½p) for a very ordinary bar of chocolate.

We were appalled.

Englishmen have complained for years about the cost of items abroad. We naturally assumed we'd be cheated.

A lurch from the train, and a fresh start, this time with an electric locomotive to take us on through Austria. Slowly the grass beside the track looked greener, more lush. The air seemed clearer, the atmosphere damper. Wild flowers in profusion dotted the fields and nearby slopes. Picture postcard Austrian scenery passing the window.

Lunchtime, but nobody ate. What point in keeping regular times in a thoroughly irregular existence? Ryvita would keep anyway. My mother, reasoning that bread would quickly go stale, had given me Ryvita, as suggested in our tour circular.

One by one we nodded off, glad of an excuse to pass the hours somehow.

The next thing I knew we reached *Salzburg*. Nearly everyone got off here. More refills or changes of water – some even washed in the cool drinking fountain since beards in the early stages itch and make you feel incredibly unkempt.

Roger Clarke, a very clever friend from both school and Cambridge – an archetypal swot – knew both the time of the train's departure and the layout of Salzburg itself. He offered to lead a small party out of the station for a quick trip to see the castle. I envied his confidence; I daren't follow for fear of the train leaving me behind. Others did wander away from the train and into the city for half an hour.

I sauntered along the platform. The booking hall was hung with flags and bunting. What were they celebrating? I felt a strong temptation to approach an Austrian girl neatly dressed in traditional costume, for information. Why not? Attractive, she was obviously there to encourage the tourist trade. Then I smelt coffee and was drawn elsewhere.

A little man in a white coat, sporting a moustache and a mountain hat in green felt, complete with a feather, stood dispensing refreshments from a trolley. The sort of character I might have photographed. It didn't occur to me that he, too, might be dressed specially for the tourists.

A large queue formed around him. In addition to coffee, you could buy chocolate or the trolley's speciality – greasy hot dogs scooped onto a cardboard platter with a liberal dollop of bright yellow mustard from a large tin.

My stomach said no.

As I waited, I began to rehearse the German sentence in my mind: *'Ein Kaffee mit Zucker, bitte.'*

I was so surprised: the man understood me and handed me a cardboard cup with gusto. I paid in German Marks because I'd brought no Austrian Schillings. Energetically, he counted out my change: 'Ein Mark, zwei Mark, drei… seben Mark fünfzig. Danke Schön.'

He beamed and immediately turned to his next customer with equal enthusiasm. My turn to do calculations back on the train. I'd been swindled! That coffee cost me about 1/9 (9p, perhaps). Back home, you could get three halves of bitter for that.

Oh well, the Englishman abroad…More proof that foreigners were out to exploit us.

★★★

As the mountains began swelling around us, we ran into wet weather again. For me, the natural fortresses of the Alps were a novelty. I stood for some time in the corridor, overwhelmed by splendour. I'd never seen clouds hanging so low; they seemed to cling to the sides of the dark rock. Chris Elston and I, both keen photographers, guessed the

exposure and took pictures from the moving train of various mountains louring over the brilliant grassland.

Great pine woods chased each other down the mountain sides. Occasionally a castle overlooked the valleys.

A turbulent, muddy river swayed with the bends in the track. Railway and river both in the valley. I'd never seen anything like it.

'That's probably a glacier stream – judging from its colour,' James said. Quiet, inscrutable, he was a scholar from Eton; his friend Chris Hall, also at Kings, was older, having already done National Service. Quiet, both be-spectacled, self-contained as a pair.

The two became experts at this stage – map unfolded, looking out for landmarks, they were following the train's course.

It seemed the train cared nothing for our admiration of the scenery. With a sudden lurch, it swept away a view, leaving us staring at blank rock, and opened up a vista on the other side. So much to wonder at: snow on some peaks, even at the end of July. Constant reminders we were passing through skiing country.

'Badgastein – that's a holiday resort,' James said.

Again we saw the formality of the railway hierarchy. Each time the train went through a station, however insignificant, the station master stood stiffly to attention, a strange baton like a solid tennis racquet under his arm. He didn't move as we were hurtled away from him.

The train seemed slowly to be climbing; soon, inevitably, the long tunnel closed around us. We had to break through the Alpine barrier somewhere, though the engineers seemed to have postponed that plunge into darkness for as long as possible.

'We've just come through the Tauern Pass,' Chris Hall said.

Of course, I thought, that's why it's called the *Tauern* Express.

All jokes at home of a *Tavern* Express and a resident bar through to Athens had finally been shattered.

Villach was a small place, the last town in Austria before we brushed aside the Iron Curtain. We arrived there at about 9.30 PM. The remains of light were slipping from the sky. Apprehension began building in the compartment. Still the time of the Cold War. The brusque unpredictability of Communist officials was proverbial. We knew our propaganda. Uneasy, I began to check I had my visa and passport.

They'd gone! I'd had them in my back pocket. What had I done with them? I began checking in my rucksack up in the luggage rack.

'They shoot you for less than that, Richard,' Chris Hall said.

The rails squealed beneath us; the train groaned to a halt.

'This is *it*, chaps.'

A hush settled over the train. Distant hissing, some panting from a steam engine somewhere. I began to get anxious, searching more frantically. Then at last I saw the precious documents nestling down the back of the seat – just visible. They'd worked out of my hip pocket during one of my dozes.

'Oh, thank goodness,' I said aloud.

It wasn't the end of the known world. Not yet.

An Austrian official, in a neat dark-grey suit, smiled and passed in the corridor. The last send off, and the change of engines. This was the last of smooth electric traction through the mountains. From now on, a burly locomotive, more smoke than steam, would take us through Jugoslavia.

A faint whiff of sulphur in the air as if we'd reached the entrance to hell. The Commander warned us that Jugoslav locomotives burnt cheap coal and produced foul-smelling smoke. We'd suffocate if the windows weren't closed through tunnels. We lurched off again, a steady canter downhill towards Jugoslavia. All seemed highly symbolic. On both sides of the track, forbidding woods: the trees, clustered together, frowned down on the train.

'Look out! A tunnel!'

Clunk went our window. For a second, yellowish smoke swirled at the glass, and then we were enveloped by blackness. No lighting. Nervous giggles from various parts of the coach.

'This is good propaganda,' someone said.

Di DUM, Di DUM. The wheels clattered; the blackness seemed interminable.

Suddenly, Jugoslavia.

After all the build-up, there seemed little difference from the other side. A factory went by, with the lights on, smoke curling out of its chimney.

'Poor devils,' someone said.

'Isn't it depressing?' said another.

Couldn't see it myself, but I said nothing, wondering if we'd entered Jugoslavia determined to see squalor and unhappiness.

The train ground to a standstill at the border station. Several people on the platform stared at us. Were we that different? Before long, an official appeared, a huge sheaf of forms in his hand. He, too, wore light grey – discreet, ordinary.

'Just look at the poor material in that uniform,' Chris Hall said.

What did it matter what we came out with? He couldn't understand us. Voluble in his own language, to us he uttered no more than bull-like grunts. 'Wog-baiting' became our only form of retaliation. At home we still respected authority. David Frost, our contemporary at Cambridge, would soon launch satirical attacks on the Establishment and change our world for ever. Still, we knew naturally we were superior to this lot; foreign authority, anyone officious, became fair game – a target for our baiting.

But only when we knew they wouldn't understand us.

The forms were in duplicate, and we were required to state in full what items of value we had, what currencies we were carrying, and in what amounts. I couldn't resist putting down that I was taking Five pounds, four shillings and a ha'penny into the country. Our signatures on the forms bound us to take everything out again, too. All, that is, except the Jugoslav *dinars* which they were keen for us to spend while we travelled through their country.

After a certain amount of pen-borrowing, the forms were complete. The door slid back with a crash and an official glowered at us.

We stared back.

'What's he want? Passports or these forms – the contremarques?'

Seeing someone holding the dark blue book, the man stretched out his hand.

'It's passports he wants.'

Still trying hard not to laugh.

Merle and Janet stood tiptoe on the seat to get their passports from their rucksacks overhead. A second official mysteriously appeared in the doorway and let off a volley of Serbo-Croat, gesticulating violently at their feet.

'Who's he think he is? It isn't a Jugoslav coach, anyway.'

We decided not to argue when we saw a holster and truncheon slung from his belt. Armed police – an unnerving novelty.

We waited ages. The meticulous rigmarole of collecting forms and stamping visas and passports dragged on. The official scribbled on each one personally as if checking the items.

'Never mind, it's good bedtime reading for some high-up tonight.'

'What is this place, anyway?'

No name board anywhere. The station seemed soulless as well as nameless. The clumsy roof structure was supported on utilitarian concrete pillars.

Chris Hall put his head out. 'Do you know, they're having an organised sing-song up here – near the front of the train.'

'What?'

We could just hear sounds of singing from some distance away.

At last, the train moved off. Almost dark now. We couldn't see much of the country. There seemed to be very few houses; beside the track, a narrow road chased in and out of bends in an effort to keep up with us, its surface an eerie glow in the rain which had settled into a steady pour. In the distance, towards the outline of some foothills, sullen clouds squatted. Terrific flares of sheet lightning jumped from one to another, but we heard no thunder.

Our thoughts turned into the compartment again, and we began eating, having waited until after the excitement.

The door shot back violently.

'Passpor..' rasped a voice.

The official wore dark glasses and a white peaked cap. He seemed particularly aggressive and peremptory.

We hesitated and then relaxed. Nobody moved; we just grinned.

David Groves, one of the larger party, had better luck next door. He collected all the passports from the Commander's company before he was recognised. Our leader, the incarnation of efficiency, had been deceived.

The first stop was *Ljubljana*, and, through the rain and darkness, we heard animated voices. My seat was next to the corridor. Easy for me to go and look outside. All along the platform, hundreds of grey, rain-soaked soldiers clustered, clearly intending to come aboard. Most of them must have been of National Service age. One climbed into the train and thrust down a corridor window with force. Bag after bag of luggage was passed up to him. Laughing and chattering, the soldiers began crowding along the corridor. Down went all the blinds of the English compartments as the young Slavs peered in hopefully, looking for a seat.

They were friendly enough and started joking with me. I struggled, feeling inadequate. Couldn't understand them.

'*Sprechen Sie deutsch?*' I ventured, remembering that Jugoslavia once learned German out of necessity. But they were too young to know much about the war; some looked younger than me. A murmur ran down the corridor when they thought I was German. They too had their prejudices.

'No, no, I'm English,' I said.

Their faces relaxed, broad smiles again.

'Yes? No?' said a particularly wide set of teeth.

Friendly enough, but clearly not much chance of conversation. No point in staying with them, so with a smile I dived back into our compartment.

Nothing to do but wait for bed-time. Cut off from other compartments by the young soldiers outside, we seemed even more isolated. At the other window, brilliant spreads of sheet lightning and cool sulphurous air blowing in; on the corridor side only a faded green blind as a barricade against the boisterous laughter-makers.

At 10 PM we began piling the luggage on the floor, keeping our feet on the seats. My lilo went on top and we managed a platform bed, level with the seats. Only the really scrupulous bothered to force their way to the washroom past the still exuberant soldiers. Besides, the onboard taps had stopped supplying more than a drip or two and an enthusiastic gurgle.

Merle and Janet, the two Newnham girls, climbed up into comfortable isolation in the now empty luggage racks. The remaining six of us settled down in head-to-toe formation across the seats and the raft of luggage. Sardines in a tin. We took our shoes off and stowed them somewhere. The pair of socks under my nose weren't too unsavoury, but I felt a pair of knees in the small of my back. We couldn't move much beyond an occasional wiggle of the toes and a wave with one arm. A choice of two positions: either with our heads flat and our knees up or straight legs and our body in a semi-sitting position.

Through a tiny crack in the blinds I could see the grey uniforms of the soldiers. Quieter now, they were leaning heavily on the window bars along the corridor, trying to sleep standing up.

James was asleep already and began to encroach on Chris Elston next to him. We grinned at each other in sympathy, and Chris looked at his watch. Just the blue night-light, the warm compartment. One by one we closed our eyes and gave up the struggle to wait for morning.

At some point I jerked awake. 'This is impossible!'

My voice woke the others. The air, thick and heavy, clung all round us, oppressive, unpleasant. The sliding window, with a will of its own, had shut itself when it thought we wouldn't notice. We wanted fresh air overnight even if it meant sulphurous smoke as well. Now the compartment felt stiflingly hot.

Somehow, we tied the window open and settled once more crosswise over the seats. Conversation again subsided to a murmur.

I sighed.

The long night's journey into day.

Now I was One and Twenty...

Saturday August 1st
Three hours' sleep perhaps, then all six of us stirred simultaneously. My head felt thick through lack of sleep, the stubble of my new beard scruffy; a dull ache in the crook of my knees.

Three days of waiting for something, the next stage our only way of measuring the journey. We waited for bedtime; then, when it came, the long haul, waiting for morning. Now we longed for *Belgrade* – the capital of Jugoslavia; the soldiers outside waiting, too, as their impatient chatter from the corridor told us.

August 1st – Chris Elston's twenty-first birthday. I planned to buy him some wine in Belgrade; we'd have about an hour's wait before the train departed. Wine was special, sophisticated – the stuff of formal dinners. *We* knew beer, not wine. Only a select few at college, like Hugh Johnson, knew about wine. I thought a bottle would be something special for Chris's coming-of-age.

I'd known him for ten years. We both came from the London suburbs and started at a well-known London school as scholarship boys, after passing the eleven-plus examination. There we began a new life, following the same academic courses through school and college.

But there the similarities ended.

Chris was more sporty than me and represented the school at both Rugby and Cricket. He became Captain of School as well. Restrained, thoughtful and utterly reliable, Chris seemed a natural establishment man – a safe pair of hands who went on to a distinguished career in the Bank of England. Compact emotionally and in stature, he epitomised the schoolboy hero: good-looking, strong-chinned, and with a flair of reddish hair, which hinted at stronger emotions than he ever let us see.

The train pulled into Belgrade at about 6.15 AM after an approach beside tall, featureless buildings and a long bridge over a grey river. No worse, probably, than some of the slums of London, but depressing to someone seeing them for the first time. A city turns its back on the railway, and few places look their best from a train.

The platform was alive with people, and our soldiers repeated their bag-hustling through the corridor window. We capitalists clustered at the windows ourselves, eager for the first glimpse of a Communist city and its inhabitants.

Merle now decided she'd come alive. Up in the luggage rack, she raised her tousled head from her makeshift pillow. She liked her sleep as much as we later discovered John did.

Over the next few weeks, we came to know and mimic his refrain whenever evening tiredness overtook him: 'Come on, lads, how about some kip?'

That morning John made some sarcastic or envious comment which upset Merle.

'Oh, don't be cross with me!' She pouted as she swung her legs earthwards. 'I can't help it.' We all resented at some time that dark curly head's ability to sleep through the demands of even the most insistent customs official.

It seemed best to take turns to look round outside; the Commander warned that, in spite of reserved seats, our compartment was likely to be invaded by Jugoslavs if we all went exploring together. Insistence and pushiness were Slav virtues – necessary since The People's supply of trains and carriage space was limited. We saw one train leave Belgrade with bodies crammed into every conceivable space. Each compartment had at least fifteen people inside, and one woman, unable to board the train any other way, was lifted bodily and bundled through an open window just as if she was baggage. Others clung precariously to the high-stepped running boards of the train. Even so we could see happy faces. Sounds of laughter and singing floated across to us as that train edged out of the station.

Definitely not English…

Those of us on guard duty first spent our time controlling *our* inrush of new passengers by attempting to recite the word for 'reserved' which appeared on our seat reservation tickets.

No one understood us.

I tried another tack: 'Bezet, Bezet,' I insisted. I'd noticed this word showed in the aperture of the door along the corridor when the toilet was occupied, and so I hoped the invaders would understand. It didn't make much difference; still they probed our defences. The word was probably Flemish.

Several people from our party went off to see something of the city, there being no official check of incoming or outgoing passengers at the station. Wander off and wander on. The rest of us took turns to step down onto the platform and enjoy a splash in the drinking fountain. Our carriage was still waterless and likely to remain so, the toilet bowl fouled and crammed with paper – quite unusable. I cannot imagine how we coped. Several brave males claimed they made discreet use of open windows to have a pee once the train was moving.

At last my chance came to slip off in search of wine for Chris. I soon found the station restaurant, dark and cheerless as were many station restaurants then, even at home; it was also early in the morning. Just inside the entrance, I found a huge bar – open, even at that hour. I tried French first: '*Bouteille de vin?*'

The burly man just stared at me.

I didn't know whether he understood or not. Gesturing with a surly thumb over his shoulder, he motioned me deeper in, towards the main part of the restaurant. Curious, I looked round. Nothing particularly unusual about the place. Natural, I thought, for the carpet strips to be Communist red. A little hesitant, I stood at an intersection waiting for attention, and before long a waiter was at my side.

'Do you speak English?'

'Non.'

'French – *français?*'

'Non. *Deutsch.*'

The German words for 'bottle' and 'wine' vanished from my memory, and I began to flounder.

'Can I help?' said a female voice.

A good-looking blonde uncrossed her legs and got up from a nearby table. She explained she was Austrian, spoke German but could understand English as well. I wondered afterwards what she was doing there so early in the morning. Perhaps waiting for more than a train. No such suspicions crossed my mind then. Just glad of the help.

I explained I wanted some white wine, and she proceeded to talk at length to the waiter. Apparently, there was some difficulty which I couldn't understand. Wine was a Continental thing, I thought; naturally Jugoslavia would have a thriving wine industry. Eventually a full dark green bottle did arrive. I examined it in the hope of recognising its contents, but parts of the label were torn away.

I looked up and saw the waiter shaking his head and waving his hand.

Ah! Not the original bottle. In fact, the cork had been hastily pared to fit and protruded stubbily from the top.

While the waiter changed my crisp high-denomination *dinar* note, the woman explained why it looked odd. They'd had to find a suitable bottle to fill from a barrel in the kitchens.

Thanking them both profusely, I walked out, clutching my prize and headed back for the compartment.

'Er – Happy twenty-first birthday, Chris.'

I thrust the bottle awkwardly towards him. No wrapping, of course.

He stood the bottle upright out of the way since the cork looked none too secure – the official celebration saved for later. I wasn't the only one to give him a present: Roger Clarke gave him a small propelling pencil.

Still some time left of my 'spell ashore', so Janet and I ventured out into Belgrade itself. Can't say I was familiar with her. We knew the names of most female Classicists of our year. Janet was quiet, self-contained. Merle was different – notable for her name and her good looks. She seemed to have something French about her, perhaps because of her first name. We speculated more than once in college what exotic background she came from: her surname Tong even suggested some trace of the orient, but her face looked very English.

Janet and I didn't know which way to go outside the station. Just an aimless wander, then – a little walk in both directions. Very little colour out there: square utility buildings, office blocks, maybe five or six floors high, the occasional older house. An overall impression of greyness. Occasional brightness, a yellow van, perhaps, or dashes of post-box red against the grey cheerlessness and untidiness. A considerable amount of mud and dust outside, roads of uneven cobbles. It was all like a model for Orwell's 1984. Poverty or neglect? I couldn't tell.

No need to keep to the pavement. We wandered at will. Little traffic about: a few ramshackle cars and buses, battered and shabby like the surroundings. A horse slow-clopped across the cobbles drawing a rickety cart, laden with baskets. Everywhere dull and dispirited: people and places aren't at their best in grey morning light.

Intrigued and repelled, Janet and I found a good vantage point for a general photograph. I needed human scale and interest. Eventually a drab little sweeper, trailing a besom behind him, walked into the picture…

We were reluctant to go further away from the station – always the nagging fear that the Commander might be wrong and the train would leave without us. I felt uneasy. It wouldn't be pleasant being stranded in a country that already showed unwillingness to welcome visitors. A few years later, another friend from college, Jim Peers, drove across Europe to Greece and spent an unpleasant night in a Jugoslav jail after some minor traffic incident in which he wasn't to blame.

Janet and I picked our way over the cobbles back to the station and penetrated the gloom of the entrance hall: we had to pass through a wedge of men standing on the steps and out into the street. They stood there gesturing towards anyone carrying even a small parcel. I had only my camera, and I wasn't letting anyone carry that. All so different from home. Feeling guilty, I sneaked a photograph. I could only conclude this soliciting, this vying for attention was a desperate response to being unemployed.

Others in the compartment now took their turn at exploring. Janet and I climbed back onto the train and resumed the task of repelling boarders. The corridor was rapidly filling up. I stood in the doorway of the compartment smiling and making suitable *Bezet* noises. I wasn't sure they believed me, but they couldn't physically shift me. Outside, also, the platform was crowded – clusters of people, talking and laughing amongst themselves. Happy people in cheerless surroundings.

At last, everybody returned. Now people could see our compartment was full.

Little England.

The train dawdled after Belgrade, taking more than twelve hours to cross the country and reach the Greek border. Austria had revealed spectacular scenery: here the countryside became deeply rural and uninteresting. Chris Elston reckoned they grew nothing but maize. The train chugged South and East, rolling sulphurous fumes across the fields or through our window. We passed small villages. Like going back in time: the roads were muddy, the people frequently barefoot, always in drab clothes. Before this day, *peasant* had been a term of light abuse we used amongst ourselves.

Now we saw the real thing.

A long day. Nothing to do. When conversation dried, we tried to read, or dozed, disconsolate. At some point I got into an adventure – the first of this holiday.

I stepped out into the crowded corridor, probably exchanging a few remarks with Roger Clarke or others in nearby compartments – some of our larger party.

Soon I found myself in deep conversation with Tatiana – a beautiful, dark-eyed Jugoslav girl with shoulder-length black hair. She was standing in the corridor, leaning on one of the window bars. A student, and going to Athens, too. Perhaps she spoke first.

Amazing to find someone who could speak fluent English. Immediate rapport. Did we just get talking or were we drawn to each other? I didn't know if others were with her; both our worlds melted away once we got into conversation. The universe contracted to one window and a support rail to lean on in that corridor. Facing each other in intense isolation for several hours and many miles, we enjoyed long, urgent conversations.

Like the archetypal Englishman, I mentioned the weather: 'Did you see the thunder and lightning last night? It was very powerful.'

Tatiana looked blank.

Stupid, I thought, how can you see thunder?

I tried again: 'Last night – very powerful – thunder and lightning, er…' My mind raced. '*Donner und Blitzen.*'

'Ah,' she said, '*grmljavina i munje.*'

She had very white, even teeth.

'What is that?'

She repeated it: '*Grmljavina i munje.*'

'Grom…' I tried.

She laughed. 'It is very difficult language for an Englishman, I think.'

She took out a notebook, licked a pencil and wrote the words down. Her writing looked thick, forceful, sloped strongly to the right. No words remotely like Latin, Greek or even German.

How on earth do they pronounce five ugly consonants together, I wondered.

Dark hair, white teeth, full lips.

We could talk, it seemed, about anything. I'd never experienced such intense closeness and interest in me.

The countryside passed us by, oblivious.

A small mole on her neck drew my eye, emphasising her smooth olive skin. She was beautiful.

Somewhere between Belgrade and Skopje I fell in love with a Slav girl – a Communist spy, for all I knew, and dangerous. For her, though, I would cheerfully have become 'the sixth man'. Tatiana – the very name promised mystery and adventure. It spoke to the heart of me. We shared much eye contact and concentrated talking – Lewis Carroll stuff: of thunder and lightning, jellyfish and things.

Somewhere in *Kosovo*, Chris took a picture, but I had eyes only for my dark beauty. Other loyalties tugged. Our group had been told that Jugoslav restaurant cars served excellent food at inexpensive prices. One or two dining cars had been coupled to our train. We'd obtained *dinars* at home for just this occasion and looked forward to one proper meal on our journey. A welcome in Jugoslavia for tourists, at last. The others from the compartment assumed I'd join them. They clustered in the corridor and looked inquiringly at me.

Reluctant, I looked at Tatiana and shrugged, then went along. She stayed behind.

We found the dining car clean, basic and modern. Very welcome after the squalor of our own coach. Several of us went through and sat in fours at the bench tables, neat with white cloths. Luxury. At home, dining cars were posh and for first class travellers. I'd never been in one before. The impression of brightness was enhanced by the appearance of the sun. For the first time since we'd left England, the sun came out – hot and bright through the picture window. White tablecloths, maroon upholstery, we relaxed into comfort. The Commander was right: we enjoyed a good, filling meal in that restaurant car.

'Must do this on the way back,' John said.

'Yeah, if we can afford it,' I replied.

'Save our *dinars*, then.' Chris, ever cautious with money.

But, as it turned out, before our return, several people needed to change their *dinars* into *drachmas* to ease cash shortage in Athens.

The train idled along in the hot sun, cutting deeper into hilly country. Frequent tunnels now. After lunch, I dallied with Tatiana during that long afternoon, close in each other's space.

'Will you swim in the sea when you get to Greece?' I asked.

'Oh, yes, I look forward very much to warm sea, clear water. It will be new thing for me.'

I tried to imagine her in a swimming costume. Black, I was sure, emphasising her height, her slimness.

She ran her fingers through her dark hair, briefly forming a pony tail, then let it sway loose again. Her dark eyes held me.

I swallowed.

'I imagine there will be jellyfish in the warm water,' I said. 'Do you fear them?'

'Jelly fish?'

'Yes, they float in the water –' I gestured with my hand – 'may be dangerous. They can sting you if you touch them.'

'Ah, *meduza*,' she said.

'Medusa, is it?' I replied, remembering the Gorgon of mythology with snakes for hair.

'It is not *meduza* I fear in the sea. It is the *morski jež*.'

'Oh, what is that?'

'*Morski jež*? I do not know how you call it in English. It very painful if you touch it with your foot.'

What on earth could she mean?

The train started to slow down.

'Look, will you excuse me a minute? Are we coming to a station? I don't want my friends to think I've got lost.' Artful dodger, heart in the corridor and head in the compartment, I left her a while to resume contact with the others and regain myself.

An hour late at *Skopje*.

Many travellers got off here, making the train less crowded. The city left no mark on my memory at the time – just another bloody stop. But four years later almost to the day, an earthquake destroyed it. It killed about 1100 people and made 120,000 homeless. Then I remembered – Skopje – we'd been through there.

At last, 9.30 PM and the Jugoslav border. Twenty-four long hours to cross that conglomeration of states. Time for that celebration. Chris had saved my gift bottle until now. Each of us tried some in a cup or a mug.

Something extremely odd about the taste. The clear liquid had a strong smell, looked very pale, almost colourless.

'Cheers, Chris, Happy birthday!'

'Cheers, everybody. Goodbye, Jugoslavia. Here's to Greece and a good holiday.'

We all took a sip.

It tasted absolutely foul – like nothing we'd ever known before. Dry, fiery. Few people finished it.

'Yes, well, I think we can say this wine has *a really distinctive taste*, Richard. Most unusual,' Chris said.

'Yes, subtle and very *distinctive*,' Mike said.

In a letter home, Chris was less guarded. '*It was disgusting stuff*,' he wrote. We blamed the Jugoslavs for their poor oenological skills.

But was it wine we drank that night?

Years later, I discovered the flavour again and realised what we'd had that evening. It wasn't wine at all and definitely an acquired taste: *Slivovitz* – brandy made from plums. Bitter and very dry. Not surprising I'd been sold this in Belgrade. Jugoslavia is home to more than seventy-five million plum trees. They have to do something with all that produce. The brandy I bought was probably double-distilled, the national drink.

Just what a tourist would want, they must have thought.

I'd been obsessed and appalled that armed guards ranged the corridors on the train. One man hurried through the dining car while we ate. A pistol holster on the left hip and a long truncheon at its side. So unlike Dixon-of-Dock-Green England. I needed proof to support my traveller's tale when I got home and determined to take a photograph if I possibly could. We'd reached the border already – the guards would soon leave. It was already dark so I'd need the flash, but I'd have to be subtle, didn't want to attract attention or trouble by annoying the officer. Whenever I heard footsteps, I peeped out of our compartment.

Another character roamed those corridors, a Jugoslav waiter with beer to sell to any traveller who could afford it. He was a damn nuisance, a Chaplinesque character – white coat, moustache like a drooped toothbrush. Eager to please, eager to make his last few sales before he too left the train.

Utterly unable to understand anything said to him.

He stood aside to allow the armed guard to pass in the corridor. Out I popped from the compartment, camera at the ready.

'Oh, bloody hell!' I said.

The waiter obscured my view of the guard.

Mike honked his laugh. 'Oops, Jemima!' – a catchphrase he uttered whenever something went slightly wrong.

Our little waiter immediately posed for me. He saw nothing unusual about an armed guard. I clearly wanted to take *his* photograph. With chin poised proudly and two beer bottles splayed in his hand, he faced the camera with a conquering smirk.

I tried waving him to one side. Eagerly he obliged, posed and smiled. Another attempt at re-positioning him. More smiles. Reluctantly I took his picture.

'Oops, Jemima,' Mike said again.

'Hops!' the waiter said.

'Hops, *Jemima*,' Mike started to teach him the phrase. Wog-baiting had begun.

A brief ironical language lesson ensued. Laughter all round.

By this time, I wished I could shove the waiter aside rather than endure this charade. Eventually he moved away, and I pointed my camera towards the guard who still lingered near the end of the corridor. Pistol and baton just visible. With luck I could…

The waiter turned once more, and, believing now he had a fan club, posed again. Delighted puzzlement.

Couldn't take a third picture; too obvious. I cursed and subsided into my seat. Jemima, our waiter, helped pass the time, but none of us bought his beers.

The Jugoslav officials undertook an elaborate collection of all the forms they'd issued. Though ordinary people were cheery enough, officialdom was dour and strict.

Goodbye, Jugoslavia!

At last we left the sulphurous engine behind; a new locomotive steamed us on to the Greek border post at *Idomeni*.

The contrast couldn't have been greater. All the grimness of the Slav officials was left behind now. A new people, different temperament. Suddenly we were aware of a warm night and crickets singing, opened up to the congenial atmosphere of friendliness and freedom. *Greece* at last. No urgency now to collect and check passports; the currency officials equally lethargic. Everyone took their time – the *laissez faire* approach of Greek officialdom, which charmed and irritated us over the next few weeks.

More washing in the drinking fountain at Idomeni – the train's WC still seized up and waterless. Both Mike and I were slow to think of settling in the compartment.

The corridor was quieter now. Tatiana still lingered; still we talked. Mike joined in.

'We are not in a hurry to go into our compartment to sleep,' my tones deliberately measured. 'It's very hot and cramped. Horrible.'

'There are plenty empty compartments now. Back there,' she said. 'Look, I show you.'

She took me back down the train, showed me where she'd be. Ideal – the sort of space John and I enjoyed on the first night.

And it would prolong the adventure.

'Yes, OK, I'll join you soon.'

I don't know what kind of invitation it was – hardly a sexual one on such a crowded train, I guess. But others commented on how she and I were getting on very well together. Tatiana was my age but had the instinctual knowledge of centuries on her side. Was she recognising our rapport, or just being helpful? Certainly she seemed keen to assist others by passing on information: even The Commander started looking for an empty compartment.

'*Now I was one and twenty…*' as the old verse goes, but, even so, still a virgin – mind and body.

Sometime in the next hour, I got cold feet. Did I lose courage, did Mike talk me out of it or refuse to join me on the adventure? Did he say, 'You don't know her, you don't want to go off on your own, etc, etc'?

Did the idea of sharing accommodation suddenly seem absurd?

I left Tatiana that night talking animatedly to people in Serbo-Croat about sleeping accommodation. Expecting me to join her.

I didn't. I'd like to think I went down the corridor and saw others with her in that compartment. Strangers.

Cowardice or commonsense made me crawl back into that stuffy compartment where eight of us slept – or couldn't, and where the window closed when it felt like it. We didn't sleep; Greece was all around us now, and the temperature in the compartment was insufferable.

Later, Mike and I went out into the corridor again, whispering and watching night-time activity at *Thessalonica*. The train lurched forwards and backwards several times. Shunting coaches, presumably. With prejudice fully primed, we muttered to each other about this typical display of Greek inefficiency.

I never spoke to Tatiana again, saw her only once on the train next day. She didn't notice me or seek me out. Somehow I knew she was ignoring me, deliberately not seeing me. The previous day hadn't happened.

Always ready to take on guilt, I felt rebuked, shrank into myself. A promise I hadn't kept. I assumed she slept alone in her compartment that night, waiting for me.

But maybe it wasn't important.

For fifty years I've pondered from time to time what was going on between us. Still something stirs. Had I really betrayed her, or did I let myself down, by not saying yes to life and those dark eyes?

The Most Beautiful Women We'd Ever Seen

Sunday, August 2nd
We awoke cramped and grumpy after our last night on the train. Sunday morning: we'd been travelling together since Thursday afternoon and were impatient for *Athens* now. But time didn't matter to the train; it bumbled southwards, at least an hour late.

The country where we'd stay for the next month showed dry and bare – browns and yellows, reddish rock. Very little grass – such arid landscape a surprise. The sun grew hot early, making the window rails in the corridor almost unbearable to touch. Leaning out of the train at 7.30 AM, we gauged the temperature to be well into the 70s Fahrenheit. At first, we travelled through high country, the train weaving round the side of mountains or tunnelling through them; eventually vast chequered plains opened out, and we had our first sight of Greek peasants working in the fields, or with their mules, carrying packs or baskets, slung pannier-style over the animal. True beasts of burden. Occasionally an old woman, in drab colours and muffled up against the sun, barely aboard her mule, slouched side-saddle and took her time in the heat.

These people seemed small in the vast landscape, part of a great oneness in the universe: heat striking up from below to link with the heat of the big sky. In this closeness to the earth, in the hot sun, the people seemed to embody primitive contentment. Already I'd noticed a difference in culture: they covered up against the sun; we began quickly to shed our sweaters, travelling jackets. Not yet in shorts, though; I still wore baggy khaki drills – ex-army stock – a sudden must-have fashion in our first year at Cambridge. No jeans then for young people.

Eventually, we came into straggling suburbs; everywhere so dusty; and at last, we had a distant view of the *Acropolis* away on its hill above the modern city – tiny, like a model. Finally, about midday, we reached ΣΕΚ, (SEK) the main railway station for travellers from the North. We heaved out into hot sun on an open platform and walked some way down to a covered concourse. Bustle and confusion, of course: our large party milling about, and another, also from Cambridge, shortly to return home – on our train presumably, but not, I hope, before they'd properly cleaned and serviced it.

I had a surprise when a member of the outgoing group sought me out: 'Are you, Pike? There's a letter waiting for you back at the hotel.'

Dear Rich,

Heaven knows if this will find you…

The rest of the family were about to go on holiday, so my mother wrote an early letter to me at the Rex hotel where I said we'd be staying, concerned to attempt some contact with a son who seemed half way across the world, as she saw it. France she knew, Germany, perhaps, but Greece…

Good to establish the link. Family tradition then was that letters to and from abroad took forever to arrive and could scarcely be relied on. Annoying, then, to find the letter reached Athens before me. Air mail was still a new thing.

Letters and postcards would be our only link with home. We'd never have considered a phone call except in a real emergency. But contact was possible. We learned of a *Poste Restante* service at Cook's in Constitution Square where letters from home could wait for us. A useful arrangement since we'd be travelling about but would often return to Athens before setting off again.

We staggered out of the station and into that wall of heat. The glare of the day struck up from the bright dust. Was it really a good idea to dispense with sunglasses? Everywhere we looked, Athenian men in shirtsleeves were wearing them.

The arrangement was that a couple of taxis would carry our luggage across the city to the three places we'd be staying: just like university, there'd be careful segregation of the sexes. The girls would stay at XEN (YWCA) and the males in two cheap hotels. Only on the train did we learn that the *Rex* hotel hadn't room for all of us, so they'd booked some of us in at the *Olympus*.

I'd expected ramshackle jalopies for taxis such as we'd seen in Belgrade. Far from it! The Greeks drove plush, American limousines with pride – clear signs of post-war modernity and renovation. A relief to be able to walk without packs on our backs. We set off from the station in a straggling English crocodile, anxious not to lose sight of the leaders who knew the way. I found it difficult to keep up and gaze at the new city at the same time.

XEN was extremely modern and comfortable. The girls would be staying in luxurious surroundings. Anxious to attract tourists now, the authorities had made this basic hostel smart and attractive. Cool stone, polished floors. Strange to find it in *Homer Street*. The poet belonged in our Ancient World, not this modern one. Glad to get briefly out of the heat, many took advantage of ice-cold water from the drinking fountain in the lobby.

'See you on the train back,' someone called as Merle and Janet walked off.

A brief glance over their shoulder: already preoccupied, they ignored our farewell.

Now, time to find *our* accommodation. So began our long trek. The *Rex* first, where most of the party were staying. The Commander still led the way, wanting to ensure we were settled. At last I could retrieve my mother's letter.

Then, on from the *Rex* to find the *Olympus* Hotel. On the way, a chance to view one of the squares Athens was most proud of 'OMONIA, *Concord* or *Harmony* Square. It wasn't long before we christened it *Ammonia* Square. Nothing so clean and smart as this in central London. It wasn't a square at all. I was reminded of Piccadilly Circus, but that couldn't touch this for brightness and modernity. This had grass, and in the centre, high fountains flared in a hexagonal lake, spraying more water than any we knew in London. Below ground, approached from all sides by wide escalators from the street, more polished stone – marble, perhaps – the main metro station down to the Port.

Eventually we arrived hot and weary in *Piraeus Street* – one of the older and busier roads in the city, the above-ground way to the port of Athens.

'This is it – the *Olympus*,' said someone, reading the Greek lettering.

But it wasn't for us. The hotel keeper denied all knowledge of our booking, and we were left on the street. Perhaps he didn't like the look of students, hot, dirty and weary after three days' travelling. Apparently, Greek hotels were notoriously unreliable.

'I suppose they think they're doing you a favour if they take you in,' someone said.

We had a problem, but *we* couldn't solve it. All of us were too hot, too tired to care. The Commander worked his passage that day, desperately trying to find accommodation. We had our baggage with us now; it had been dropped off outside the *Olympus*, the taxi long gone. We waited submissively in the heat, sitting on our baggage, again drinking water. An anxious time.

'Soon have to take a salt tablet at this rate,' James said.

Listless, passive, we believed dumbly some solution would be found.

Slowly, a crowd of Greeks began to gather, eyeing us up and down as we sat outside the hotel on the pavement. Soon there was a Babel of suggestions for our welfare. Good to hear one woman speaking English. Eventually we learned that the Lux hotel had been persuaded to take us.

'How many?' said Chris Elston, already suspicious of Greek hospitality. We didn't fancy the group being splintered further.

'How many you want? He take two, four, eight.'

We relaxed; just six of us, the group from King's. Still together, still being herded. Back across town again, lugging in the heat. Ironic, really: the Lux Hotel was practically next door to the Rex where the other men in the party had already settled.

The Lux was a category D hotel, of a similar standard to a British youth hostel. Staying there would cost the equivalent of about 5/-(25p) per night.

It would do. Like beggars, we couldn't be choosers.

We went in off the street. No cool marble here. We tramped steadily up two flights of stairs – a tall, narrow, unkempt building, stretching back from the road. On the first floor sat an old woman on a kitchen chair. She nodded as we passed.

Concierge, I thought, trying to be sophisticated about hotels.

The rooms had three beds each. A quick division into two groups of three: Chris, Mike and I in one room; Chris Hall, John, and James went to another. Thankful to have found a place, we slipped our rucksacks to the floor. Simple essentials only: the floorboards were bare and splintery; old fashioned, but fairly comfortable iron beds made up with just two sheets and a pillow. The window was between two of the beds and shuttered against the heat. It gave out onto a small balcony overlooking the busy street below. Like typical English, we flung the shutters open to let light and street noise in. Shouts, cars hooting. Sudden glare. And the smell on the air – something which came to epitomise Athens for me – the smell of restaurants, grilled meat, especially.

Inside, flies danced and spiralled round the light. Steady heat. We chose our beds. Someone tried the wash basin.

'There's no hot water.'

'Well, I shan't bother shaving, then. Have to grow a beard.'

'Where's the bog?'

Down the corridor, towards the back of the building. Another basic amenity: flies darting, circling, the strong smell of urine lingering. Just as well we'd brought our own toilet paper.

I still had food left from the journey. I didn't fancy it, not now we were in Athens. A quick wash and out for a meal. Find a restaurant for a late lunch.

'I know what I'm looking forward to,' said Chris. 'Must have some melon.'

We all agreed, must have melon. A new thing for us. A luxury, if seen at all in England.

Over that holiday we had our fill of melons, sometimes having them every day. Interesting to learn the two different words. It seemed strange at first. To us melon was melon. We had the yellow, fleshy sort that day – πεπονι (it seemed to be pronounced idiomatically *peponyi*) and that probably became our favourite. Later, as confidence and *savoir faire* increased, we tried the huge red-fleshed water melon – καρπουζι (karpouzi), sometimes sharing a whole one between us.

We found a place that appealed and all six of us sat down for our first meal. We had great difficulty getting what we wanted, however. Our knowledge of Ancient Greek was not a great help. We could read the words on the menu, but didn't know what they meant. Even the common words for bread and water had all changed. No one understood our efforts. The waiter did his best: he spoke Greek and a little French. Fortunately wine hadn't changed; we could say that in Greek or French. He brought us a thin yellowish liquid, cheap and resinous.

'This must be Retsina,' someone said.

A custom that puzzled us at first, but became very welcome, was that wherever we ate or drank, they always served water. Whether you had melon, bread, coffee, or lemonade, always they brought a glass of beautiful, cold water. One day while we sat at a pavement café, a passer-by paused at a nearby table, said a few words and helped himself to someone's glass of water before continuing on his way.

Not English.

'Where do they get all this water from?'

'Search me. You don't see clouds in the sky, and they don't have rain.'

'Well, not in the summer, anyway.'

Over our meal we tried to decide what a typical Greek looked like. Not much success there. Once we'd got past the dark glasses and white, short-sleeved shirt, the only common factor seemed to be dark hair. It didn't take long to decide, though, that Athens was the place with the most beautiful women we'd ever seen. We out-numbered girls eight to one in Cambridge and there was always strict segregation of the sexes, except in lectures. Here was heaven. We saw more attractive girls per hundred yards than we'd ever known before. As clean-living young men of the 1950s, we were in a permanent state of 'Arry Frusters – the old forces' slang still lingered. We were readily drawn to these girls with their dark hair and dark eyes, all of them extremely buxom. I noted that Greek girls seemed to develop at about ten or eleven, and many were quite happy to catch our eye and flirt. They tended to find us most interesting when we wore shorts. Couldn't understand why.

Occasionally, we saw a blue or grey-eyed girl and that seemed to make her even more attractive. Blondes were rare. Typically, we never looked at the older women to see what our goddesses grew into.

In spite of our lack of sleep on the train, we were not yet tired. We'd have a nap later, probably, but before sleeping we decided to try a short walk to the Acropolis.

Athens had altered while we ate. Now it was truly the heat of the day and everyone seemed to be taking a siesta. Very few people around – only mad dogs and Englishmen.

Incredible how dusty Athens was. After the Second World War, the Greeks had endured further fighting against the Communists. That was one reason why the resumption of the Olympic Games took place in England in 1948. Although the obvious symbolic choice, Athens wasn't safe. The vast rebuilding plan had started some thirteen years previously, and the regeneration programme was still under way: new buildings and civic amenities, pavement re-laying, road works everywhere. Construction work always creates dust. Afflicted by heat *and* the building work, Athens was dry and very dusty. It quickly became clear why there seemed to be shoe cleaners on every corner. We liked to watch a business man stop, climb up a step or two onto a seat and sit, like a monarch on a throne, while some lackey knelt before him to clean and polish his shoes.

'Try it,' John said one day. 'Have a go, Chris, let the chap clean your shoes.'

'But I'm wearing sandals.'

'Give it a go!'

It wasn't a total triumph as Chris revealed in a letter home: *Sandals a great success and very relaxing. They've changed colour slightly because one great oaf in our party with the initials JBB insisted I had them cleaned when a little shoeblack boy came up to us while sitting at a table drinking beer under the Acropolis. Actually I think they look better now.*

We knew the rough direction for the ancient Greek citadel, the Acropolis. All six Kingsmen set off in a loose straggle down a broad main street. Not much traffic, fewer people. Silence settled in the heat. We, of course, walked on the sunny side of the street. None of us wore a hat.

From across the other side of the road, someone wanted to attract our attention: 'Cou, cou. Cou, cou!'

Six heads turned to look.

An old woman, her back close to a doorway, sat in the shade on a low stool. Sure of her audience now, she grasped the hem of her skirt in both hands and wafted it up and down. Legs apart, offering the dark mysteries of the female sex.

'Cou, cou. Cou, cou!'

Six English heads turned resolutely to face the front; upper lips stiffened. We walked on. A definite reaction of surprise amongst us, but we never discussed the incident.

Instinctively I understood it to be a sexual invitation, not for herself – that was out of the question – but pimping for hidden delights in some upper room behind her. I was as innocent as any then, but somehow felt I'd come across such an un-English overture somewhere before. I could only think of the novels of Simenon.

Though I said nothing to the others, after that, I viewed the concierge on the landing at the Lux with more suspicion than I'd done previously. Folklore among us now says we were staying in a brothel…

I've never again seen such a primitive and blatant gesture and wonder now whether the woman was giving an elaborate insult to foreigners in her city, like the open-palm flinging gesture we'd been warned about. Certainly there was nothing enticing or attractive in her display.

We finally reached the foot of the Acropolis. Above us, the Parthenon and the Erechtheum, both scarcely visible close to. Before us, a steady climb up a broad marble-slabbed path to the Propylaea, the gateway into the old citadel. Here our courage failed. The heat struck up from the bright stone, polished by the feet of centuries; the temperature now oppressive. We'd found it; that'd have to do for today.

We wandered slowly back to our hotel, taking time to look in shop windows. Half-past three now: we were ready for that nap and all slept through until dinner-time. Anxious not to pay for two restaurant meals in a day, we decided to eat up the remaining food from the train journey. Then we went out.

The sun set quickly at about 7.30 PM. Dark now. We searched out a café where we could have a drink: clear fizzy lemonade, with, of course, a glass of water.

The day's exertions had left us thirsty, possibly dehydrated.

'Anyone else want another?' Chris said.

We all agreed we did.

Not so easy. We had great difficulty making

the waiter understand what we wanted. He seemed to think we were haggling over the price. Neither French nor English worked, not even a smattering of German. Should we just pay up and shut up? Eventually a solution, amid laughter and curiosity. Not for the first time that trip, we relied on sign language and mime to convey what we wanted.

At last, we got our second lemonade.

Finally, happy and contented, we walked down the darkened streets of the city. Athens was alive again, people out walking, even young children.

It wasn't long before we were greeted in English by a stranger – Greek warmth that we experienced more than once in the capital.

Writing home the next day, I commented on this:

The wogs themselves are friendly – extremely so. Twice already people have come up in the street, said 'Are you English?', made polite conversation with us, told us we're very welcome and wished us a good holiday, and, with a handshake and a smile, disappeared. [In their own language] they seem to jabber and we can't understand them, though they do understand our Greek…

I blush now at the way we behaved in private. We often found Greek talk difficult and blocked it out when we could.

'All this bloody Yakkabakaka,' Mike said – an expression he'd culled from *The Goon Show*. Often we were mistaken for Americans; the greeting became even warmer when they learned we were English.

But we did make some effort to learn basic Greek. By breakfast next morning we knew that νερο κρυο (nerro crio) was the inevitable cold water.

The weak electric light in our hotel made the room seem faded and brown. Hardly welcoming. I had with me an electric razor I'd bought from John at college. I tried once more to get it to work by poking the bare wires into the one electric socket in the room. I quickly gave that up; I'd already had one belt of a shock.

Have to grow a beard, then. Wondering what I'd look like, I decided not to tell my parents and see how they reacted on my return.

We soon settled down for our first proper night in Greece. Not much talking after lights out. A good sound sleep, though I did wake up hot and perspiring and longing for a drink. Had to wait, though. Wouldn't dream of drinking the water from the tap in the basin. Before I set out, my mother regaled me with horror stories of her student days in the 1920s when she'd toured rural France with a friend. I was able to add a reassuring postscript to my letter home: *no* bedbugs.

★ ★ ★

Monday August 3rd

We awoke to the sound of traffic funnelling up from the narrow street. All of us were hungry now. No breakfast in the hotel: we'd have to go out. Already we'd settled naturally into our group of four; Chris Hall and James went off on their own.

At first I thought the meal odd, but eventually came to love it. We drank delicious cold milk – with the glass of water – and an interesting mixture of honey and butter to spread on soft, new bread. We soon learned to ask for βουτηρο-μελι (voutyro-meli) wherever we went, but it was always at its best in Athens; the thought of that tangy, dark, liquid honey from Mount Hymettus, mixed with fresh unsalted butter, still makes my mouth water. Simple but delicious.

As always, we chattered away in English with unguarded comments. Why not? Who'd understand us? Two people at the next table were talking animatedly in Greek. But slowly, strangely, English words began to creep into their conversation. Eventually their speech changed entirely into English. These strangers turned out to be Greek Americans who'd returned home. Like all Athenians, they happened to be very friendly and offered help. The first thing they did was to check our bill to reassure us it was accurate. We were paranoid about being cheated. το λογαριασμο (to logariasmo, the bill) was fine and we began to relax. The men then went with us to show us the *Hellas* restaurant which they recommended. Another problem solved. We knew now where to eat in the evening.

Away they went, leaving us glowing at their friendliness and kindness.

Immediately afterwards: 'Hallo, boys. How are you? Amerikani?'

'No. Angliki.'

'Angliki, huh? Let me shake you by the hand.' Another man greeting us enthusiastically, one by one. 'You very welcome here. We pleased to see you.'

Unbelievable, such open warmth. We marvelled afterwards at the welcome we'd received.

'You wouldn't get us greeting foreigners like that – not in London.'

'Definitely not, everybody's pretty cold and reserved, by comparison.'

We were falling under the spell of Greece and its people. Magical moments like this later drove us to see films like *Never on Sunday* and *Zorba the Greek* – anything to renew acquaintance with the warm, eccentric people we'd encountered and came to love. I wonder how long before the people of Athens stopped greeting English tourists with such openness. We decided then that we must be benefiting from the legacy of what the British had done in the war.

We spent that morning on a guided trip round Athens, learning the ropes, getting our bearings. Cashing travellers' cheques was a lengthy process – the bane of English holidays abroad for years. We found Cook's in Constitution Square for the *Poste Restante* and began also to distinguish the Tourist Police – a force which seemed strange to us, familiar only with British bobbies who directed traffic, solved crimes, and would even tell you the way or the time. The Greek Tourist Police were scattered throughout major holiday areas, assigned supposedly to helping tourists in distress or with problems. We encountered them occasionally over the next few weeks. They must have been at least bilingual. Ideal, really, to have such a force, but I later heard them described with less enthusiasm by female visitors to Greece as 'lecherous Dutch uncles.' Quite often during our holiday, we approached them with a question only to be answered with an eloquent shrug.

We were still tired after our journey and returned to the Lux for a long siesta. Chris and John woke first and went out for a trip to the Acropolis – Mecca for any classicist. Mike and I were left to sleep on; I also wanted to write a letter home, and my diary. Anxious already to capture as much as I could of what looked like being a great adventure, I needed time to write, even if only in notes. Trouble was I wanted to write three times as much as the others and often had to cut my writing short because we had to press on.

About five o'clock, when some of the heat had lifted from the day, Mike and I strolled off for a lemonade and ended up sitting in the gardens of the National Archaeological Museum. This modern building, built in classical style, houses one of the world's greatest collections of sculptures and vases, covering the full range of almost three thousand years of Ancient Greek Civilisation. We didn't go in – it had already closed for the day – but it gave opportunities for camera-clicking wonder at the neo-classical buildings, or ruminative philosophising such as Mike and I often indulged in.

We all knew about Lycabettus. It always seemed strange that Athens had a mountain within its boundary. The Acropolis was just a hill by comparison. Both geographical features were clearly visible from certain vantage points around; from Lycabettus we knew there'd be good views over the city.

After dinner at the Hellas restaurant and hoping to see the sun set, we set out for a brief assault on the mountain. We hurried away from the restaurant, and walked up the steep hill from the XEN (YWCA) to begin climbing steps up the lower slopes. The buildings now looked more elegant: huge blocks in modern styles; it was obviously a more prosperous area. We were in a hurry, knowing the sun would soon disappear behind the ring of mountains to the west, long before all light went. Unfortunately, we didn't know the best route and ploughed up amongst the pine trees, weaving in and out, trying desperately to find the path that'd make progress easier and lead us to the top.

Eventually we found the wide, shallow-stepped slope, but knew now we'd never reach the chapel and the top of the mountain in time. Somewhere from a clearing, I just managed a picture of the sun feebly glowing orange before snuggling into the mountain haze. Within minutes it was dark.

Both Chris and I tried another picture now: guessing the time exposure, I steadied my camera on a rock. I could see bright dots of light below us. That picture emerged later as faint smudges in the blackness. Chris's exposure was more accurate and achieved something of the magic.

Athens settling into night.

A Touch of the Exotic

We'd been brought up on schoolboy ancient Greek and needed to make rapid adjustments in our attempts to read the words all around us. No one actually knew how the dead language was pronounced; the Greek letter beta (β) we'd always pronounced as a B; here in Athens it was pronounced as a V. So the mountain we'd scrambled up at dusk was actually Lycavettus to the Greeks. But the language couldn't make do without the B sound. That had to be reproduced by two letters together: M and P. Anyone wanting an alcoholic drink had to go into a MPAR. It wasn't long before we'd christened any bar we saw an *oompah*. On the entrance door of one, I saw the Athenian attempt to woo the tourists: MPUSS. Being indigent and clean-living young men, we rarely *pushed* open the door of such establishments.

They couldn't say 'shoosh' to us either. The Greeks didn't have a letter for it.

It became a source of delight to see how the Greeks recreated English words in their own spelling. The Ch sound as in 'chin' couldn't be reproduced by their letter χ (chi); that sound was more guttural and back of the throat as in the Scottish word *loch*. One of the streets of Athens had been renamed in honour of Churchill. The great man's name became transliterated so that it read Tsurtsill; in a nearby cinema I noticed also they were showing films in which Tsarli Tsaplin starred.

There was always a lot to wonder at. In the restaurants we sampled Greek coffee and ate Loukoumia. At home we might have called it Turkish Coffee and Turkish Delight; here it wasn't politic to do so. The coffee was very strong and very sweet, a mere mouthful in a small cup and a great deal of sediment; it didn't seem aesthetically pleasing or value for money. Mud at the bottom of the cup.

We soon stopped ordering it, and, whenever we saw Νεσκαφες (Nescaphes) on the menu, we ordered it, preferring the more predictable instant coffee, even though it was expensive. *Loukoumia* appeared occasionally as an end-of-meal delicacy. The subtle rosewater or citrus flavour of the pink or yellow jelly, and the powdery, flavoured sugar which dusted the little cut pieces, was always welcome. Sometimes chopped nuts were embedded in the sticky squares. I enjoyed the sweet and already planned to take five boxes of it home as presents.

It's amazing now how thrilled we were to find delicious dessert grapes in the restaurants; like melon, this often became a must-have. Were they really such a rarity at home?

As a real treat, we liked to find a Ζαχαροπλαστειον (Zacharoplasteion) and discover the delights of Greek pastry and cake-making. Sometimes we had pastries for pudding in a restaurant. I took to several of them, particularly καταιφι (cataïfi) which resembled a Shredded Wheat biscuit, stuffed with nuts and currants and, always, swimming with honey. The other, baklava, was similar, except that layers of filo pastry separated the nuts and currants. The delight was to watch it ooze honey when you cut it with a spoon or fork. These pastries can be found in England now, but nothing can match the impact of this totally new cuisine on our starved and simpler palates. I salivate as I recall them. We were kids in a sweet shop and often crossed the road to investigate, or clustered round the shop window whenever we saw the sign for a zacharoplasteion.

At the time we believed all this new food was specifically native and the Greeks would certainly boast it so. We didn't realise then how many unacknowledged culinary transfers there were in that region; Turkey and Bulgaria both have similar cuisine. Moussaka is now a supermarket ready-meal; then we believed it was an archetypically Greek dish. We made sure we sampled it, but the bitterness of the aubergine in the dish wasn't always to our taste.

We had to adjust also to how the name of the dish was pronounced. None of the languid English 'Moussa*rk*a' here. We quickly learned to ask for '*Mouss*akka.'

John was the first to enthuse about ξιφιας (ziphias, swordfish) and soon others tried it, only to rave about a taste and texture totally un-English. Eaten with *Tsips*, it was delicious, better in memory than any swordfish steaks available now in this country. Perhaps it was because they cooked it in butter.

Whenever we couldn't get the waiters to understand what food we wanted at restaurants, we were often invited – or made our own way – to the kitchen at the back where we just pointed.

One dish did become a favourite: we knew it wasn't Greek and tended to be expensive, but it was new to us – Wiener Schnitzel, or, as the menus called it, *snitsel*. Totally unavailable at home then, and still is, largely, but now more for animal welfare reasons than scarcity. We loved the crisp bread-crumbed steaks and the lemons they provided as garnish, made sure we chose it whenever we wanted a treat, such as our last meal in Athens before returning home.

We tried *retsina* – that peculiarly Greek white wine which is very much an acquired taste. The practice of putting pine resin in white wine during fermentation dates back to Ancient Greece. It was intended to preserve it, but in many ways the wine tasted worse than the vinegar it would have become if left untreated. It gave the wine a bitterness that took some getting used to; someone once described it as tasting like turpentine. Now, if you look for it and really want to drink it, you'll find it on supermarket shelves here.

We knew about the Greek spirit *ouzo*, too, but on our limited budget, we didn't try it often. Another acquired taste. On the rare occasions I drink it now, I take it neat. I can't say it appeals as an aperitif, or after a meal. The aniseed flavour is pleasant enough but hardly seems to go with anything else. But I was fascinated then to watch Greek men pour water into the spirit so that it swirled with milky clouds.

We'd brought our Anglo-Saxon ways with us and often preferred beer rather than wine. We soon discovered Μπυρα Φιξ (Mpira Phix) in bottles. No doubt we complained about its fizziness – it was a Greek version of a German beer, made under licence – but it tasted refreshing and we must have coined the expression 'having a Fix' a few years before it acquired more sinister connotations. On special occasions we sampled Greek Brandy – *koniak*, as they called it, which, with all the snobbery I could muster, I drank readily enough but despised – because it wasn't the proper stuff. Cheap, though.

Walking around Athens we were fascinated to see street sellers swathed in huge bundles of sponges. At home, sponges were neatly round or square, definitely synthetic, and in lurid colours. You bought them from a chemist. In Greece they were pale yellow, misshapen and decidedly organic.

'They're the skeletons of creatures that live on the bottom of the sea, aren't they? Don't they have to dive for them?' John said.

'I thought they were vegetable and you grow them,' I said.

'That's loofahs isn't it?' Chris added his wisdom.

'Maybe. Perhaps these are plants that grow in the sea, like seaweed.'

None of us knew. I certainly bought one to bring home, used it to rinse myself in the bath, marvelled at how much water it would hold. Occasionally I sniffed it, sure I could still detect the tang of the sea.

'Everywhere you go, you'll see an awful lot of kitsch,' the don, Norman Routledge, had warned. 'Terrible stuff. Don't waste your money.'

I didn't know the word, but I soon realised what he meant when I saw the bad taste souvenirs available from stalls near Classical sites or from specialist tourist shops in the city: poor imitations of Ancient Greek pottery, in black and terracotta; misshapen statues of well-known Greek gods, all grandeur and dignity gone; painted plates with famous views; Greek temples, or models of the Parthenon – maybe even in a snowstorm…

But by the end of the holiday, even we cultural snobs had succumbed to something which took our fancy.

Positioned strategically along the main streets of Athens were kiosks selling almost everything: newspapers, maps, films, postcards, of course – and tobacco products. The kiosks were festooned with their wares and often drew us just to look. The owner was deep inside as if in a military pillbox.

A Touch of the Exotic

Some of us started flirting with smoking at Cambridge, but no one would have called himself a smoker. I hadn't yet taken up pipe-smoking as a principal hobby – though I certainly started at Cambridge – otherwise I'd have chuffed my way round Greece.

We decided we'd try Greek cigarettes. Again the comparison with Turkey loomed, the taste and smell being distinctly Middle-Eastern. A touch of the Balkan sobranie, or the tobacco *latakia*. More and more I began to see Athens as the halfway point between East and West. Certainly the strangely modulating music that accosted our ears from time to time seemed more oriental than Western. Nothing Lonnie or Tommy or Elvis would ever sing.

We managed to avoid beedies – peculiar little smokes, of cigarette length and size, but hollow and dark brown, which had the pungency of a bad cigar. After experimenting with stronger flavours, we settled on *Papastratos Ena*. Number One – the mild one. Just a touch of the exotic: we agreed they tasted rather better than a Gauloise. We all bought a packet at some time and offered them round. Another post-prandial delight, relaxation at the end of a busy day sight-seeing.

Any tourist going to a Classical must-see country is faced with confusion and culture fatigue. In Italy, for example, all sense of history is lost as one journeys round to gawp at the different cultures. Roman, Etruscan, Medieval, even Greek remains are there, and often close to each other. Here it was just the same: the Classical stuff which we knew about and had come to see, but also during our time there, we encountered Mycenean civilisation, Minoan civilisation – both from earlier Greek times. But the situation was confused further by many Roman remains, and evidence of a culture I knew nothing about: the Byzantine. We couldn't avoid it and eventually included it in our itineraries, but privately I tried to block out any personal response to a culture that had come from Constantinople/ Byzantium/ Istanbul.

For me it was foreign and brought cultural overload. We'd not been taught about the Byzantine Empire.

So I made up my excuses and couldn't be doing with anything else…

The Trials of Spending a Drachma

Tuesday, August 4th

Our sight-seeing began. Delphi was to be our first destination. Back in England, we'd opted for a coach trip laid on by the organiser as an extra. Already the large party had fragmented into smaller groups: some had set off for the Peloponnese, the hand-and-finger-shaped rest of mainland Greece; others to the Greek islands, or to Crete. We'd save those for later. The bus was at our disposal and stopped several times for us to view sites of interest on the way. We didn't reach Delphi until late afternoon.

We knew Delphi was important. It featured often in the Classical literature we read – history or tragedy. Of religious significance rather than military, it clung to the lower slopes of Mount Parnassus, itself a sacred mountain and dedicated to Apollo. Ancient Greeks believed Delphi to be the centre of the world and called it, picturesquely, the navel ʼομφαλος (omphalos).

The place was famous as the home of the Delphic oracle, and anyone who wanted to know the future, or whether an enterprise was auspicious, would send an envoy with gifts in order to consult the Pythia, Apollo's priestess. She was ensconced deep in the inner sanctum of the temple and sat on a tripod stool over a mysterious fissure in the rock. From here sulphurous volcanic fumes seeped up and intoxicated her. Any words she uttered in her trance were completely incoherent, and needed – of course – to be interpreted by priests nearby. In religious or moral matters the oracle was supreme, giving good advice to any questioner who'd sent to the oracle to ask how best to avert evil and be reconciled with the gods.

In more secular matters, particularly those where self-interest was concerned, the oracle's responses were often ambiguous or riddling, leaving the questioner, just as the Three Witches left Macbeth, with an answer that could be shaped by his own wishes and interpretation. So the word *Delphic* came to be proverbial for an obscure or enigmatic answer.

One example from the sixth century BC: King Croesus, he of fabulous wealth, was King of Lydia in Asia Minor and planned a punitive expedition against the neighbouring country of Persia where Cyrus was king. Cyrus had driven Croesus' brother-in-law from the throne of Media and annexed the country. He had to be punished.

Croesus sent generous offerings to Delphi asking whether his proposed trans-border expedition would be a success.

'If King Croesus crosses the River Halys,' came the reply, 'he will destroy a great army.'

Croesus was overjoyed at such a positive response and made immediate preparations for war.

He did cross the River Halys; and he did destroy a great army.

His own.

After that, Lydia, too, became subject to the laws of the Medes and Persians.

It's interesting to realise how widespread the Delphic Oracle's fame became and how much influence it wielded. It gathered extraordinary wealth, and several Greek city states kept treasuries there, adding to the splendour of the place by displaying their gifts to Apollo in miniature temples on the hillside. The oracle's influence lasted well into Roman times, but generally by about 400 BC the rationality of the Athenians had consigned consulting the oracle to ceremonial practice rather than something of true religious significance.

Even so, terse wisdom comes down to us from the walls of the Temple of Apollo. The walls have long gone; the sentiments have not. Inscribed there were two precepts, still applicable to modern times: Μηδεν 'αγαν and Γνωθι σεαυτον (mairden agarn and gnoethi seauton) *Nothing in excess* (or *Everything in moderation*) and *Know yourself*.

We'd heard of Delphi, then, and knew we had to go there. We clambered aboard the single-decker bus, hefting our rucksacks with us. We'd left the *Lux* hotel behind; tonight we'd sleep somewhere else, possibly in the open. We travelled now in our group of four, but the coach had several other members of the main party.

It's over a hundred miles to Delphi from Athens; the tour buses now take three hours for the journey. Ours was supposedly a luxury coach which cost us 18/6 (just under a pound) and took four hours. The terrain has dictated for years where the roads go in Greece. Not surprising, then, that we came across names of Greek city-states we'd read about in our Classical studies. Strange to find a city of myth and legend – Thebes – still exists in a modern incarnation, but sounded like Theevai to our ears. You might just as well think of seeing a signpost to Camelot somewhere in the English West Country.

We didn't realise it at the time as the bus swung round a corner, but we passed through the place 'where three roads meet' where Oedipus of legend fatefully met and killed his father. Something the Delphic oracle had predicted for him. He journeyed on from that encounter, answered the Sphinx's riddle at the gates of Thebes and became King – and married his mother…

First stop on our journey out was *Daphni*. We'd no idea what to expect; we just went where the bus took us. It was our first look at Byzantine architecture. By the end of our stay in Greece, we'd become very familiar with the architectural signature of Byzantine churches and monasteries: a red-tiled central dome and rounded arches which formed doorways and windows – buildings from the 10th to 12th century AD, unlike any Christian churches we'd ever seen. Warm and friendly churches outside, all bright stone and terracotta. Inside, however, very gloomy. The windows were small and let in little light – but equally it was a welcome respite from the heat of the day.

Overhead, a painted figure glared down from the ceiling.

'That must be Christos Pantocrator,' said someone who knew.

'Makes you think, doesn't it?' John said.

This was no 'gentle Jesus, meek and mild'. Here, staring fixedly from the central dome, was Jesus-who-ruled-everything: long, dark hair and beard, drooping moustache and severe expression. A shock to those brought up on the Victorian Protestant tradition. The eyes were harsh and judging. No kindness there. The figure glowered down. It shocked me, and I felt alienated when faced with a totally different concept of the Son of God.

Our second stop was *Eleusis*, originally 10 miles North West of Ancient Athens, now incorporated into the suburbs. We'd expected great things of a place which featured in our reading: the place of the Eleusinian Mysteries. Perhaps, at last, we might learn its arcane secrets.

What we found were just a few ruins of the temple complex once sacred to the Earth goddess Demeter – the whole site overlooked by nearby factories. For me, Classical sites became increasingly disappointing. So many were piles of stones, outlines of old buildings, the occasional standing column – little to spark my imagination. I wonder how many Classicists feel the same.

The bus also stopped at *Osios Loukas* – a shrine sacred to Holy Luke, the hermit, not Saint Luke of Gospel fame. Holy Luke founded a church here in the mid 10th century AD. This monastery, about sixty miles from Athens, is noted for its outstanding mosaics and unique position. A few monks still live here, and the place has increased in significance, especially since the hermit's remains were returned by the Vatican in 1987. But sadly to all of us now, the place is only a haze in the memory.

★ ★ ★

Delphi at last – in the heat of late afternoon. At that time it was still a village, but even so, used to catering for tourists. Our first impression was of a hillside laid out in terraces since earliest times. The road through was scarcely wide enough for two modern vehicles to pass. As we approached, the mountain loomed craggy, grey and hostile to the right of us where the main site clung to the rocks in the full sun all day. Down the hillside below, a scatter of olive trees, boulders and various other Classical remains. At first it seemed

almost haphazard, but a definite track wound up in a slow zigzag from the road towards the main site. The most fascinating thing was the distant glint of the Gulf of Corinth in the haze below and a strange dark green mass in the valley which seemed to flow down towards it. Very hard to make out what it was – probably a huge olive grove, though it didn't seem silvery enough for that.

We were dropped off late afternoon and knew we'd be around Delphi for twenty four hours, when the bus would return to pick us up. The village straddled the road: red-tiled roofs, stuccoed houses. Steep steps up or down from the road seemed the only discernible form of street, apart from the main road which passed through.

Maybe there was a hotel – but not for us. Our only definite plan for Delphi was to visit the tiny museum and see the famous bronze statue of the charioteer. We idled around, getting our bearings.

We ate at an open air restaurant on a terrace overlooking the magnificent scenic spread below. All was well with the world.

Our abiding memory of Delphi is where we slept that night. At dusk, we wound our way slowly up the hillside, following a new

path of irregular-shaped stone blocks carefully laid over the rough mountainside. We followed a small wooden signpost to *Castalia*.

Our first night under the stars, then. We found the perfect pitch where the path

seemed to level out to a natural plateau, and a clear stream scurried down the hillside, formed a few pools nearby, then headed on down the mountain towards the road. Now well away from the village and all other civilisation, it seemed an ideal place to stay.

We unpacked our sleeping bags and I blew up my lilo. The path was newly laid and about six feet wide. We wouldn't even need to surround ourselves with DDT powder for protection from ants. We spread ourselves out in our *al fresco* dormitory. I remember sleeping quite close to a pool, enjoying the calming sound of the flowing water to my left. Perhaps I could just trail my hand in it. We used torches to settle ourselves; then the blackness of night. So many stars dotted above us; we seemed very small and insignificant, bedding down in one of the oldest sites in Greece and cradled by the mountain. Chris recalls that there were eight of us there: *four lasses on one side and four lads on t'other.* It seemed perfectly natural for us to act as unofficial bodyguards. We learned later that others from our party also camped nearby.

The next morning we four took full advantage of the running water – our first chance to bathe properly since we'd left England. We didn't trust it to drink, but it'd do for washing. I stood in the pool and splashed about, using soap to have a thorough wash, even though the water seemed quite cold. A natural pool, probably about six inches deep. Then we packed up and headed down to the village in search of breakfast, John, in jaunty black beret and khaki shorts, leading the way.

At some point, guilt and realisation struck us – perhaps when we saw that our stream fed a drinking trough beneath a large tree at the side of the main road. People and their animals could pause there for a drink. Or maybe one of us came to remember how the Castalian spring had been renowned since Classical times: we'd bathed that morning in water that the Greeks agree is the finest, purest, the most crystal clear in the whole of Greece. I remember cringing with guilt at the thought that someone lower down the hillside might get a taste of my Lifebuoy soap when they scooped up water to drink. How long, I wondered before our waste water had flowed away and purged our guilt? Another worry too: had any of us done the little boy thing and peed in it as well? Ironically, the area we chose to bed down in has now been closed to the public, ostensibly because of the danger of falling rocks.

A brief digression on toilets. We learned early how to ask in Greek for το 'αποχωρητηριον (the apochoreterion) a delightful term since it meant the 'little place you go away to'. Remarkably, few existed in Athens – surprising at first, until we realised that in the heat one sweated excess liquid off. You didn't need them. No doubt on the odd occasion we could have walked into any café, as you can now in Italy, and used the facilities there. But English coyness restrained us from going into a place we weren't already patronising, so we never availed ourselves of this. Out in open countryside, we peed without compunction if no one could see us. On one occasion, Chris even took a photo of the three us in a row against a hedge.

But I cannot remember ever having to defecate out in the open, so we must always have managed somehow. Well-known places had tourist pavilions with more up-to-date facilities, and we must have made use of those on many occasions. It was hard then,

Passing Time

and still is now on the continent, to discover facilities where you're expected to thrust a coin into the hand of some toothless old woman in order to use the toilet for a pee. In England, chaps didn't need 'to spend a penny.' It was always difficult to know how much to give; there wasn't a fixed charge such as we were used to, so we tried to get away with sneaking as few leptas onto the saucer as possible. Sometimes nothing at all. Often we were ignominiously called back if we underpaid. It was even harder to realise, when the real call of nature was pressing, how the attendant gave you only the toilet paper that was your quota. Just as well that on some occasions we'd taken some of our own.

We also learned and began to look out for the ancient Greek symbol for the toilet – three circles: ooo. We first found this sign on hidden doors aboard ship, and again our English sensibilities were offended by the toilet's primitive nature: a hole level with the floor, two foot rests and grab handles to get the angle right. Absolutely no seat or pedestal. Best avoided if at all possible. It's extraordinary that even now such facilities still exist and are considered normal in certain parts of Europe.

Ah well, the trials of spending a drachma.

Never Miss a Trick, Do They?

Greece is a country that appeals to the senses. Always plenty to see – not just the grandeur and symmetry of the ancient monuments, or the modern buildings, but the colour and light on the sea, the dark green fingers of cypress against the sky, the mountains, the wide plains. Our time there was a period of wonder and growth.

For me, the sense of smell was just as powerful and evocative as the sights. I came to love Athens for its street smells – particularly the lingering restaurant flavours, which merged with each other, and the traffic, and the dust.

But the handmaid and carrier of all these smells is the heat and dryness of Greece. In Delphi, the arid heat of midday had a stillness that held you – calming, almost healing. Sometimes even the cicadas fell silent. The time when Pan sleeps. The intense heat of Greece brought out the smell of the pines and flavoured the air of that midday stillness. It rarely happens in England. When I encounter it on the continent now, I pause, smile, and am always lurched back. That smell which is forever Greece.

★ ★ ★

Wednesday August 5th
John's memory of the next morning is unusual. He maintained we were given a free breakfast by an enthusiastic café proprietor because Winston Churchill had been in Delphi the day before. After fifty-five years, I find this hard to believe. I think something must have got lost in the memory or in translation, at the time. We were lucky to be given free food, and probably because we were British, no doubt out of residual admiration for Winston Churchill – after all there was a street named after him in Athens. But it seems hard to believe the great man, now an ailing eighty-four-year old had come to this remote, steep region the day before. We all saw Churchill the next year when he came to lay the foundation stone for Churchill College, one of the first new colleges to be built in Cambridge since the war. He was then rheumy and lame, struggling to walk even with a stick. By special dispensation, his car was driven right into the centre of the college grounds to get him as close as possible to the Provost's lodge.

I can still hear the provost, Noel Annan's, greeting: 'Hull*o*, Sir Winston!'

Is it possible that the lame, infirm Churchill had visited Delphi and walked the slopes of Parnassus just before us? I should like to think so, but I doubt it.

But there may be something in it. I just remember the proprietor's enthusiasm, and the strings of Union Jack pennants hung around the café and across the stepped street. After all the area was picturesque enough; perhaps there was something worth painting…

We had until 3 PM to explore. The bus which brought us out from Athens had been put at the disposal of the party, but mid afternoon was our departure time. In those days, you didn't just go to *see* Delphi and be overawed by it; you went to live it. The terrain seemed extremely rugged and bare, almost threatening. The mountain behind, above, and around us stood granite-grey, hostile and barren. The stones were hot; the ground dusty. Lizards scuttered out of our way. If we'd looked up, we'd probably have seen an eagle or two wheeling high above. Keeping watch, like the gods of old.

A town and a tourist destination now, some of Delphi's magic has been tamed. But it still remains the most imposing archaeological site in the whole of Greece. You pay an entry fee in euros now where, without paying a drachma, we wandered at will. The amazing thing was that our time in Greece was on the cusp of being a mecca for travellers and tourists. The Greeks were not quite ready to exploit the full potential of all their archaeological remains. Their heritage was totally free as we discovered later.

The sacred site had been carved out of the side of Mount Parnassus in a series of terraces.
From the air it looks like a huge rabbit scrape out of the mountain. What better way for us to proceed than to start at the bottom and work our way up? This was our first real archaeological site, and we planned to view it thoroughly, obsessively. We were helped

that from ancient times there was The Sacred Way which zigzagged upwards from the road. To see all of Delphi it would be uphill all the way.

John quickly strode off away from us towards our first ancient building.

We knew it as the *Tholos* then – a temple from the Fourth Century BC which was unusual because it was circular. We'd been led to believe that Classical temples were usually built as rectangular structures. Here was a real temple going against everything we'd been taught.

Just as with modern churches, with their dedication to some Christian saint or other, each temple was

sacred to an ancient Greek deity or one of their attributes; you might almost say to the god in one of his or her incarnations. The Tholos was actually the Temple of Athena Pronoia – Athene Forethought.

Located roughly half a mile from the main concentration of buildings at Delphi, and positioned below the main road, the tholos was considered the gateway to Delphi. The goddess's shrine stood near but below the entrance to Apollo's.

We lingered here: Chris and I began clicking from every angle, but John, to his credit, sat quietly down now and sketched what he saw. A good artist, later a brilliant part-time political cartoonist, he worked placidly at capturing his view of the world.

It wasn't long before Mike, too, was compelled to take to the sketchbook since he'd lost his little camera near Athens a few days later. He was very upset and annoyed that he lost all the pictures he'd taken.

The Tholos temple had been partially restored. The three columns now standing had been rebuilt with modern additions to give the old stones completion and stability. Reconstruction was always a battle between the purists and the repairers. The purists preferred the stones to lie where they'd fallen or been shaken by earthquakes over the centuries; the archaeologists who believed in restoration ranged from those who created a complete replica, by using the stones that remained and adding new materials, to those who gave an impression of what the building might have looked like by doing a partial restoration, as here.

I had to keep my sacrilegious views quiet. As the holiday progressed, I came to welcome any restoration, the fuller the better. To me, so many of the ancient sites seemed no more than piles of stones, usually little more than two or three feet high, lying where fate and nature had tumbled them. I lacked the patience or the imagination to see beyond what lay there, and certainly became rapidly bored with buildings that were little more than excavated outlines or foundations.

The Tholos, however, offered me one security. It had been built with *Doric columns*. And I knew about them. We learned, probably at school, that Doric columns were the first style of Classical architecture – in many ways, simplest and best. In appearance the Doric column was chunky and unadorned. It was built of drums of stone placed one upon another, the column slightly tapering towards the top.

There was a *capital* (the top, or crown) made of a circle topped by a square. The *shaft* (the tall part of the column) was plain and had twenty sides. The Doric order had no *base* to stand on. The impression was of plain, but powerful-looking columns. Doric, like most Greek styles, looked good with the long rectangular buildings made by the Greeks.

We set off again, winding our way up from the main road, to follow the ancient sacred way.

Never Miss a Trick, Do They?

The next building we came across was *The Treasury of the Athenians*, erected sometime during the Persian Wars in 490-480 BC. Its purpose was for the Athenians to give treasure and thanks to Apollo for deliverance from two Persian invasions led first by Darius and then Xerxes. This was the stuff of legend and Hollywood: Marathon, 300 Spartans, and all that.

Now, here was something I could recognise as a building: three walls, the front being the entrance with two Doric pillars – even a suggestion of how the roof might have looked. Immediately I liked it; the honey-coloured stone looked warm, almost welcoming, and I didn't need to use my imagination. The restorers had done enough to attract the gaze of a layman. As so often in those ancient buildings, we marvelled at the size of the smooth marble blocks which formed the walls. They must have been about two foot long and perhaps a foot thick. No doubt they were hewn according to some mathematical formula which created harmony. We wandered inside the building unhindered and looked around; it was like being in a roofless stone shed. Difficult to see how the treasures given to Apollo were stored or kept safe. Perhaps there were guards.

It seems strange that these ancient buildings were totally unprotected in modern times; we could have left graffiti if we'd wished. Perhaps others had. But nobody watched us; nobody shooed us off.

We continued winding our way up the hill, looking back at where we'd just been. I paused, anxious to capture in the foreground a perfect example of the capital of an *Ionic pillar* with its more sophisticated scrolls and fluting. This was a later development in Greek Architecture and one I came to love for its more graceful appearance.

The main *Temple of Apollo*, when we did reach it, about half way up the hill, was a huge disappointment. Massive broken columns now in a state of decay – no grace, no elegance. It looked as if lorry tyres had been stacked high upon each other reaching to more than twice John's height.

We'd reached the navel of the ancient world, the home of the Delphic oracle. It was hard to believe now, so abandoned, open to the elements, and insignificant did it seem. Here the ancient priestess was hidden away in her inner sanctuary, waiting to be consulted, ready to utter intoxicated gibberish for the priests of Apollo to interpret on her behalf.

Only on the outside, facing down the valley, did any trace of graceful fluting show. These stone drums seemed to emphasise the width not the height of the column. Elsewhere, the carved fluting of the Doric and Ionic styles brought out the height and grace of columns. These, dating from the 4th century BC, looked crude and squat – mere pinky-brown stones piled one on top of another. Weather had done its worst on the porous limestone, and because Delphi is also a volcanic area, much of it had been toppled; the gods get angry. We were actually looking at the remains of the third temple built on the site.

Delphi was also a site of games not unlike the Olympic Games in that they invited

Never Miss a Trick, Do They?

contestants from all over Greece to take part. Dedicated to Apollo, they also occurred every four years and were held two years before the Olympic Games. They were known as the Pythian Games, after an epithet attributed to Apollo after he'd slain the original dragon-guardian of the site, Pytho. None of this had formed a major part of our education, and it came as a surprise to discover a stadium way up the mountain beyond even the theatre. However, the Pythian Games differed from the three other Panhellenic contests in that, in honour of Apollo, competitions in music and dance were also held.

A little further up the mountain from the temple was *The Theatre* itself. This was our first encounter with ancient theatres and we marvelled at its size and the way it snuggled into the embrace of the mountainside. It afforded stunning views across the valley of Delphi, and the steep rake of the seating caused considerable amazement. We had, of course, to test the acoustics. I puffed up the steep tiers of stone seats onto the hillside itself and looked down on the circular orchestra, the view over the valley and the tiny figures below.

The artistic competitions would have been held here. The theatre was originally built in the 4th century BC but was remodelled on several occasions since. Its thirty-five rows can seat 5,000 spectators.

We were aware now that time was against us. The bus would depart at three o'clock and we wanted to look inside the museum. I took a breathless scramble up the mountainside and had just a glimpse of the stadium higher still. Time now to make our way down, weaving in and out of stones, some tumbled down naturally by the mountain, or man-carved fragments toppled by earthquakes over the centuries. Our aim was to get back down to the road and walk back into the village to find the museum.

One aspect of transport in Greece was the use of the donkey. Both Chris and I felt we wanted to record something that was so un-English and seemingly primitive.

I was particularly pleased to be able to

get an old woman to stop and pose for me. She wore typical black peasant's dress and rode side-saddle on a donkey. She reined the beast in and stopped in the middle of the road while I took her photograph.

'Thank you very much,' I called.

The woman turned her donkey and went on her way, clopping towards me. As she went by, she held out her open palm towards me. I was appalled and brusquely ignored her.

'Did you see that?' I said to Mike. 'She wanted money for taking her photograph.'

'Bloody woman,' he said, 'never miss a trick, do they?'

I Am in Sculpture Heaven

I have always been drawn more towards sculpture than architecture, so in our brief visit to the Museum I was most interested in the show piece there – the bronze statue of the charioteer. This was our first chance to get close to an original Greek statue. It was a formal figure of a youth, himself probably no more than a teenager. Such youths would have been used as drivers in chariot racing.

The figure was damaged by time, but still moving and impressive.

I was fascinated by the greenish tinge to the bronze, the inlaid glass eyes, the stylistic beauty of something first created around 470 BC.

To think that this figure had survived for more than two thousand years! It was originally part of a much larger statue, but what we have now was found in three pieces in 1896, buried under a rock-fall from Mount Parnassus. Even an earthquake, it seems, can preserve objects. Long after we'd visited, Delphi museum underwent considerable refurbishment and expansion in the mid-1970s; it was rehoused and now has several more exhibits to attract the visitor than we saw. It would be good to visit again.

And so, in the heat of the afternoon, back to the bus. Chris takes up the story: *The coach left at 3.00 and we were back in Athens again at 7.00 PM. The driver was absolutely reckless on narrow twisting roads – really rather amusing. In the end he started singing to us over the microphone; I'd have preferred it if he'd concentrated on driving.*

★ ★ ★

Thursday August 6th

We needed to start planning ahead. We knew we wanted to go to Crete; a visit to the Greek Islands was also essential, and we'd been told that the cheapest way of going round the Peloponnese – the large mainland area south of Athens – was to hire a car and share the cost. At some point we met two girls from our party and agreed to form a *sixsome* – as Chris put it – to do the journey together. Apparently we'd be able to hire a Ford Consul, and it'd cost us about £6 each for eight days. But it'd mean a lot of driving; I hadn't the skill. I was still very much at the stage of cycling everywhere.

Only Mike had actually passed his driving test in England, John had a provisional licence; the rest of us would be passengers. But in order to be able to effect the hire, Mike would have to produce his actual licence to the car company. Nothing for it: a

quick letter home to ask his parents to send the document out to him at Cooks' *Poste Restante*. In the meantime, we'd get on with our holiday.

Chris and John became determined sight-seers and left Mike and me. To them we seemed lethargic. But we did two separate things that day, but I'm not sure whether we did them as a pair or in a foursome. We visited the Archaeological Museum, and we finally conquered Mount Lycabettus.

We knew there were two significant museums in Athens. The Acropolis Museum, on the hill itself, contained all finds and artefacts from the site. The National Museum was in the busy urban centre of Athens and a very imposing and attractive building. Even though it had been completed in 1889, to our eyes it still looked very new.

We admired the vast place with colonnaded wings either side, each given over to particular archaeological specialities, such as Greek Inscriptions.

We wondered at its modernity and splendour, particularly with its mixture of rose bushes and exotic palm trees. And that was before we went inside.

The museum is one of the world's great collections of sculptures and vases covering the full range of almost three thousand years of Greek civilisation. The beauty and grandeur of all we saw there can only be imagined. This was one place where taking photographs was not allowed: we have no record of some of the treasures seen. I've been lucky to find suitable illustrations available for use on Wikipedia. But I'd recommend anybody wanting to sample a cross-section of Greek art and civilisation to visit the museum. I was in sculpture heaven. Having won a college competition for Greek Iambics in my first term at King's, I chose as my prize an illustrated book of Greek Sculpture across the centuries. Here, in Athens, I came face to face with many statues I recognized from the book, my favourite being a marvellous bronze found in the sea off Cape Artemisium: a larger-than-life figure of Poseidon, in a pose which indicated he was about to hurl a trident at an enemy. It was possible to walk all round and view him from different angles. This figure is one of the few statues that have survived from the age of Pericles and the zenith of Athenian democracy. It must have been fashioned about 450 years before Christ.

For me he was a perfect example of the male nude. I saw him then as a middle-aged man – the beard must have done it – and I made it a private ambition to have a toned figure like his when I reached forty.

Enough said.

We also came face to face with several examples of the archaic smile, a strange characteristic of sculpture from a period earlier than the Poseidon. I seem to remember we were told at school that the Greeks back in the 7th and 6th centuries BC didn't know how to carve a face with lips closed and so even the most serious of subjects was carved with a kind of smile – almost a smirk. That seems to me now rather a simplistic explanation, but there's no doubt the smile is a predominant feature of early statues.

There's a clear example of the archaic smile appearing when there's no obvious occasion for humour or gaiety. This is the figure of the dying Trojan warrior taken from the Temple of Aphaia on the Island of Aegina. It would have been created about fifty to a hundred years earlier than the great bronze Poseidon. The Trojan seems to smile as he struggles to remove the fatal arrow.

Another strange feature of Greek stone sculpture is that it was painted. We've become accustomed to seeing bare white marble, maybe even preferring its simplicity. But it's known from occasional traces of paint that today's monochrome statues were often highly coloured.

Our afternoon called for exertion. We decided to make sure this time that we reached the top of Mount Lycabettus. Previously, towards dusk, our attempt on the summit was foiled by the rapid onset of darkness. Now we took the wide official path with its shallow steps towards the chapel at the top of the three-hundred-metre high mountain. We walked up, no doubt pausing several times to catch our breath and admire the view back towards the acropolis and the sea, or over the Athens suburbs. We didn't have the advantage of riding on the funicular railway which was added a few years later. This can only have increased the Mount's attraction as a tourist venue.

I chiefly remember the chapel of St George at the summit. We were back in the Byzantine world of severe images of Christ and a variety of icons.

It was an alien world to those of us brought up in the simpler traditions of the Church of England. I seem to remember there was one metal image or icon – perhaps it was of Saint George himself – which was often kissed by visitors to the chapel. My sensitivities were repelled, and I readily thought of germs. I remember one part of the image, perhaps the foot, was highly polished by all this frequent touching and osculation.

Years later, when I came to read Gerald Durrell's description in *My Family and Other Animals* of the devotional attention paid to Saint Spiridion's body in Corfu, I knew exactly what the scene was like and shared the Durrells' revulsion at the practice.

Perhaps I'm a Bolshie

Friday, August 7th
We were surprised to find the day had dawned cloudy. Would it rain? We didn't know what to expect of Greek weather.

Our first thought was to ensure we could begin touring beyond Athens and its immediate environs. Time to book for Crete. We knew we'd have to go by boat and that it'd be a long, overnight journey. In case the authorities wanted to check our passports, all four of us made the expedition to the agency to book our tickets. Our departure was scheduled for 8 PM on Saturday night from Piraeus. In the meantime, we had a chance to explore ancient Athens thoroughly.

The Acropolis is the magnet for all tourists to Athens. We were lucky: access was not restricted as it is now. We could wander anywhere over that great hill rather than finding ourselves hemmed in by fencing and a defined path. I don't even remember if we had to pay to go up there. It was a steep climb from the street level and we wandered over smooth slabs of stone and around rocks which may once have formed part of a building.

The huge gateway of *The Propylaea* loomed ahead like a bastion. We had to go up several steps to reach it. It was certainly true that you had to climb to reach the world of the gods.

But as you walk through, it is always the *Parthenon* that first catches the eye and attention of the visitor. You still have to walk uphill to reach it, and it waits for you a little off to the right side of the Acropolis itself.

We were extremely lucky we could wander at will amongst its massive pillars and stones. It was very important for Chris as a photographer to show the scale of the building. He could do this best by showing a human figure alongside one of the columns.

Apart from its size, one of the wonders was that it was built on a sloping site. This became particularly evident when you stood at one corner of the building and let yourself be dominated by the huge Doric columns.

I did manage to do a Chris myself and capture him photographing some of the Parthenon's grandeur.

The building itself was not the most complete of the ancient temples in Greece, but its position on the citadel of Athens, and its very size, gave it awe-inspiring grandeur.

A huge explosion of the ammunition stored inside it in the seventeenth century had blown a large section of one side of the building out. Even so we could stand and admire the thickness of the inner walls.

To think that the buildings on the present acropolis were all completed within a thirty year period – the inspiration of Pericles, the Athenian leader in the mid-fifth century BC! He employed the best architects and sculptors of his day to create *this lasting possession*, as he called it. At school, we'd studied Pericles and the ambitions he had for Athens, had even translated the funeral speech he is said to have delivered (as re-created by the historian, Thucydides) over the dead of the Peloponnesian War. We knew

he wanted Athens to shine pre-eminent over all the other Greek city states, and one way was to commission so many beautiful buildings. On a clear day, travellers returning to the port of Piraeus could see the Acropolis, standing serene and dominant above the city.

In 1959 we saw the Parthenon unrestored and, in some ways, uncared for. Certainly pollution was beginning to have its effect. Nowadays, its marble glistens brightly, a lot of it as the result of cleaning and restoration. We'd worry today about the fact that Lord Elgin dubiously acquired the marble sculptures that had once adorned the Parthenon and other acropolis buildings. The debate about whether they should be returned to Greece simmers on. Then, in 1959, we couldn't have cared tuppence that they were lodged in Britain. For certain, we thought, we were better able to look after them than the Greeks.

When you turn away from the Parthenon, the other building that immediately catches your eye is the *Erechtheum*. It's a curious building, famous particularly for its *caryatids* which act as columns and support a kind of porch or side chapel.

'Who or what was Erechtheum?' Mike asked. 'Sounds like a chap with a lisp who's got a hard on.'

Someone explained that Erechtheus was supposed to have been a king in very ancient Athens. 'Had links with the sea-god, Poseidon,' Chris added. So the temple was named after him.

'Ah,' Chris said. 'Ionic columns!'

I think Ionic columns became my favourite. They were slender and sophisticated with a simple scroll at their head. I preferred them to the chunky majesty of Doric columns of earlier buildings and thought excessive the later, florid Corinthian columns which came to characterise Roman architecture. But since buildings with Doric and Ionic columns clearly existed side by side on the acropolis – all built in roughly the same Golden Age of Athens – the two styles were obviously contemporary.

In many ways, the Erechtheum seemed a more sophisticated building than the blunt majesty of the Parthenon – and somehow more welcoming. Mike felt moved to sit down and make his own sketch of the building with Mount Lycabettus in the background.

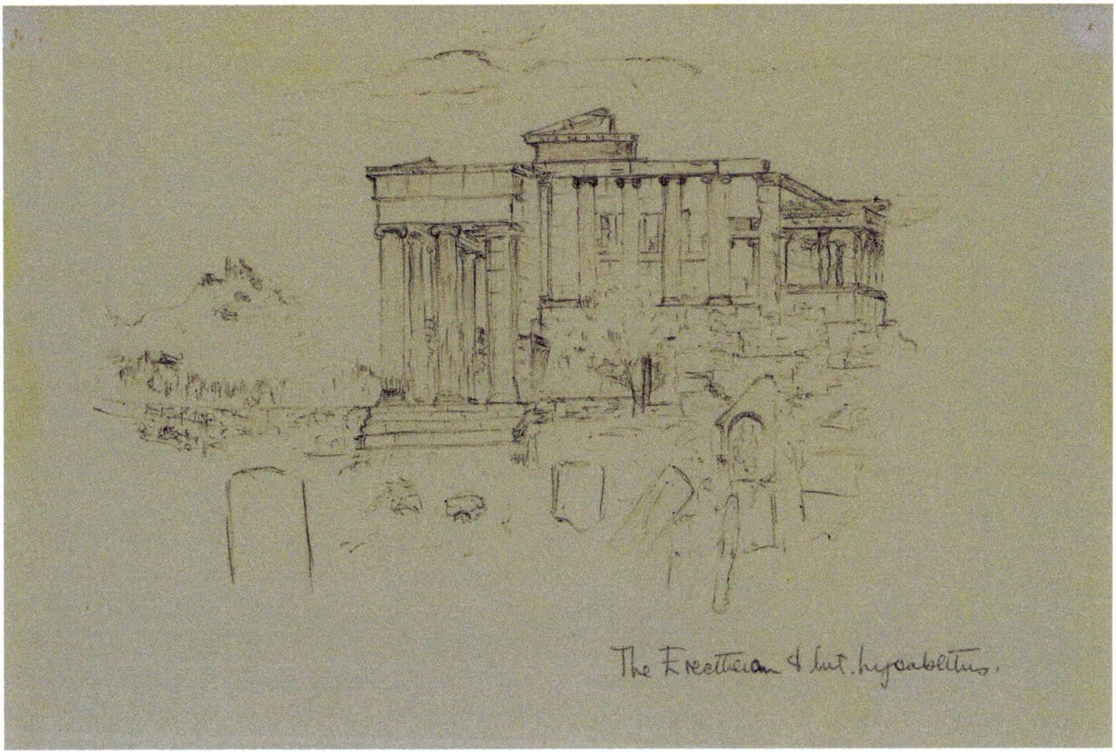
The Erectheion & Mt. Lycabettus.

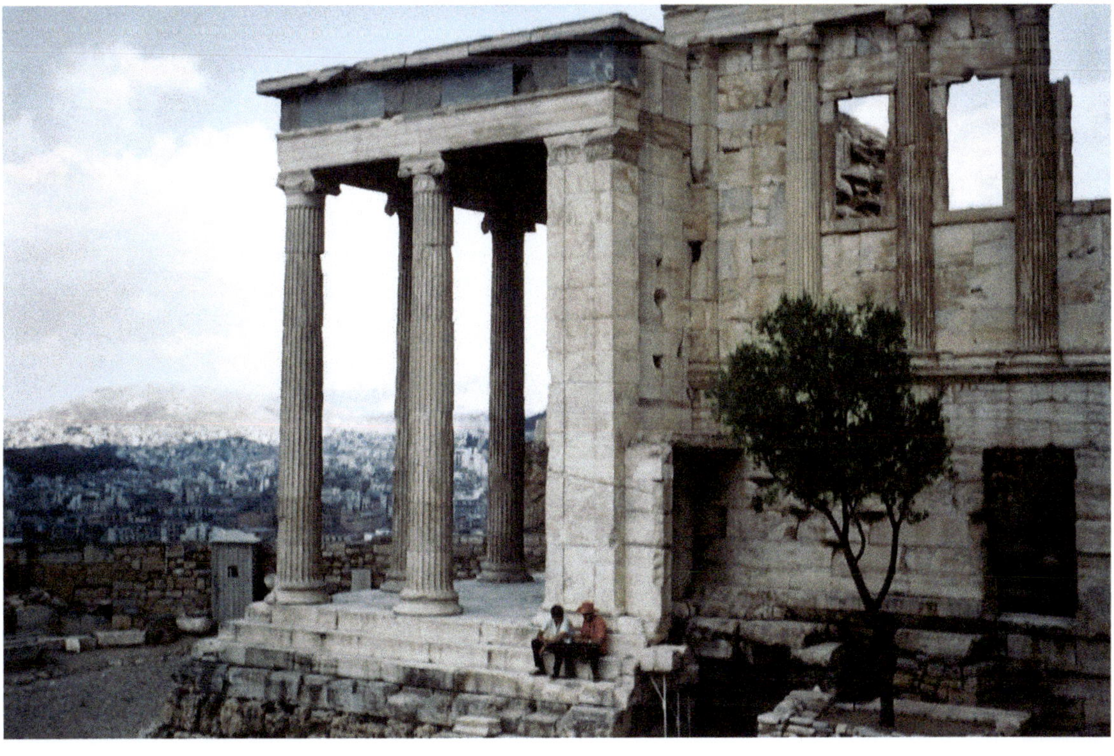

The attractive curiosity of the building was the *caryatids* which supported the roof of a porch. What we saw were all rather tired replicas; Lord Elgin had one original for the British museum; the others were preserved in the Acropolis Museum that in our day was situated in a cramped building at the far end of the citadel.

We continued our aimless wander, tiring a little in the persistent heat, even though it was cloudy. One particular attraction was the *Temple of Nike* – a small building set alongside the massive gateway of the Propylaea. Sacred originally to Athena as the Goddess of Victory, it had a charm all its own, if only because it was not a huge construction – manageable on the human scale. I'm reminded of the Treasury of the Athenians at Delphi which we'd seen earlier, though that was in the chunky, Doric Style. Ionic columns here lent greater delicacy to the building.

Tired now, we lingered on the hill and gazed down at the *Agora,* once the market area and meeting place for Ancient Athens.

Silence.

'Come on, lads, how about some nosh?' John broke the spell and began to wend his way towards the Propylaea and the long tramp down.

The Agora that afternoon was hot, dusty and, for me, ultimately depressing. It resembled a dry jumble of scattered stones and rocks at the foot of the Acropolis. No doubt there were maps and drawings of how it had once looked, but for me it was intellectually arid, and I couldn't bring any interest or creative imagination to what lay at my feet. It was a wide rectangle of devastation and ruins. Few buildings remained standing to catch the eye and elicit interest. On one side, it was hemmed in by the high cliff which formed the Acropolis; on the opposite side, a modern Metro bustled through a cutting on its way to the port of Piraeus. A modern barrier, the American Museum, was the boundary on the side which led towards the *Plaka* – the old historical neighbourhood of Athens. The *Plaka* was a place for poor tourists to find a taverna and get a cheap meal. Strangely, I don't remember us making much effort to find places to eat there.

We photographed, but ignored, the American Museum with its brash neoclassical style of Roman building. The bright terracotta tiles on the roof alienated the eye immediately. Not on our agenda at all. Equally we blocked out the Byzantine Church of the Holy Apostles which nestled at the foot of the Acropolis.

I did, however, take to the *Theseum,* as we knew it then. It was a Doric temple at the other end of the agora which looked like a smaller and more complete Parthenon. This was the first ancient building we'd seen which had any trace of the roof remaining. It is, in fact, the best-preserved ancient Greek temple in the world and is slightly older than the Parthenon. The reason for its survival in good condition is because it was kept in use as a Greek Orthodox church from the eighth century AD until 1834.

We wandered round inside the main portico admiring how the huge slabs of marble formed the roof of the building. What stopped them falling down?

I found it fascinating how the strong sunlight shafted through the gaps that did exist and lit up what would at one time have been a dark colonnade. As often with Greek temples, there was also confusion about what the building was called. Because it was dedicated to Hephaistos, the god of fire and crafts, and Athena as well, it was also known as the *Hephaisteon.* I nodded and took the puzzle no further. It can be found under either name in modern guides.

Why the association with Theseus? Stories vary. Some say his remains were brought back and buried here; others that his mythical exploits were depicted in some of the stone friezes in the temple. He was, after all, an Athenian hero and king, an early founder of Athens…

We'd decided on culture for our last evening in Athens before going to Crete: Aeschylus' *Agamemnon*. Chris and I had both read the play at school and found the language difficult, but at least we'd have the advantage of knowing the basic story. The play was being performed at the *Theatre of Herodes Atticus* which nestled on the far side of the Acropolis away from the *agora*. It could never have been performed there originally because the theatre was a Roman addition to the area.

We filed into the theatre and settled on the curved stone seating facing the stage. We'd have an excellent view of what little action there was in such an ancient play. I don't think we had any kind of cushion so the stone seating chilled and stuck to our bare thighs as the evening wore on. There would have been modern lighting, but even so I have the impression of having to wait until dusk before the play began.

'There won't be a lot of action,' I said to Mike, 'but I'll try and tell you what's going on from what I remember of the play.'

But we Classics scholars had not expected one thing, as one of my letters home reveals:

'On Friday evening we went to a restored open air theatre to see a Greek play, and they had the nerve to translate it into Modern Greek so that we couldn't understand it.

I think secretly that by the end of the five weeks I shall have had enough of this kind of holiday. It's a bit cramped living within the space of a rucksack the whole time and our hotel didn't have enough water for baths.

I personally would enjoy lazing around, learning the language and mixing with the extraordinarily uninhibited Greeks. But a certain sort of loyalty to Classics makes us press on to 'do' the classical sites. Perhaps I'm a bolshie but I don't find them half as inspiring as the others. I want time – time to enjoy the life here – my diary is rapidly going by the board because I want to write three times as much as the others – and that's only in notes.

The Acropolis with the theatre of Herodes Atticus at its foot

There is a Land Amid the Wine-Dark Sea

Saturday. August 8th
The Lux hotel expected us to pay up and check out today. This meant lugging our rucksacks with us everywhere. But the boat for Crete wouldn't leave until 8 PM. What could we do after breakfast? In spite of doubts about the weather, we took ourselves off to the seaside. We went to *Phaleron* as we called it in our Classical studies – the place where the sea came closest to the city. Phaleron was the ancient port of Athens before Piraeus was developed. Then it was basically an open site for beaching ships. This was the tenth day we'd been away from England. A letter home recalls something of that time:

Our first swim in the sea and the first bath as far as Chris and John were concerned. Funnily enough the sky has been clouded for the last two days so my tan didn't progress by the sea. It was quite warm in the water and beautifully clear. We had terrific fun with the lilo again, besieging each other and tipping each other off into the water. I spent some time blissfully lying on it, gazing at the sea bed below me.

The letter was written to my girlfriend, Meg, and I can only assume that she'd remember us fooling about with the lilo on some English beach. With all the sensitivity and gaucheness of a twenty-one year old, I went on in the letter:

The girls are pretty fabulous here and we all admit to being frusters from time to time. When I say that it is ten times as good as Edgware; you'll know what I mean. I don't think I've ever seen quite so many beautiful girls per 100 yards as there are in Athens.

As you might guess, Meg lived in Edgware…

That evening the SS Adrias set sail for *Crete*. We knew it'd be a twelve hour voyage so we'd arrive at the island in the relatively early morning. In his letter home, Chris said: *we were travelling deck class. First class was luxurious. Tourist class – they were packed in like cattle down below.* Our night was spent on deck, up near the bows *with a balmy breeze and glittering stars*, as Chris put it. I would sleep in relative comfort: in a sleeping bag and on the lilo.

I wandered around the ship before I turned in. Anywhere there was space for a human body to huddle was occupied – on seats, the floor, even shelves in open locker rooms. This was the 'peasant' class, scattered everywhere. I averted my eyes from a woman breast-feeding her child, noticed a little dog chained to a bench where his master lay. The man was shutting his eyes tight against the throb of the engines.

I walked along the deck and saw many people huddling near the sides of the boat. It worried me. I passed little children, lying on the deck for the night, some with their heads placed towards the gangway. It would have been very easy to catch them with a foot as you passed. One little girl opened huge eyes and answered my grin. Eventually, all found somewhere to snatch a few hours of sleep while the boat churned steadily southwards through the night.

★ ★ ★

Sunday August 9th
Increasing light woke us early. It was the first time in my life I'd seen the dawn.

Something to write home about: *I've just had the fascinating experience of watching the sun pop out of the sea and shine feebly and elliptically through a low bank of cloud. The sea is literally*

ultramarine in colour.' That must have been about 6.30. But we still had an hour and a half's travelling to go before we docked at *Heraklion*.

As the sun's light grew stronger, everything began to look golden, and people became restless, impatient for landfall. They wandered about. Several of them, mostly Greeks, clustered up in the bows; others stood pensive, looking over the side. As foreign travellers, we were always objects of curiosity. I came to the conclusion that none of them had ever seen a lilo before. I turned back from the sunrise to discover several Greeks bending down and prodding it tentatively.

We'd heard about Cretans wearing jackboots with a frisson of horror. Would we see any? Our associations with jackboots were all about Nazi soldiers. I even wondered if the German occupation of Crete had influenced the way the islanders dressed. Far from it: we were witnessing one or two people still naturally wearing traditional Cretan clothes. Both Chris and I reached for our cameras. Unfortunately, my camera shook in the cross wind and my excitement: my colour picture was unusable.

Here was an older man wearing part of the traditional costume: the 'βράκα' (vraka) the baggy trousers, a purple sash around his waist, the high 'jack' boots, the στιβάνια (stivania), even the 'σαρίκι' (sariki), the black kerchief tied around the head. We were seeing the end of a tradition. But by the time we left the island three days later, we were no longer so awestruck at people wearing national costume. Now, such clothes are worn for the tourists or special events, I guess.

Heraklion at eight o'clock in the morning was bright, hot and windy. We hung about for a while, watching the other passengers file off the ship. I was pleased that, in spite of a twelve-hour trip, I hadn't been sea sick. I'd had one bad Channel crossing to France in 1953, and my subsequent hypochondria had dubbed me liable to sea-sickness at the rock of a wave.

One impression of Crete was that it was much poorer, less developed economically, than the mainland.

Again both Chris and I reached for our cameras when we saw that goods were transported from the harbour by horse and cart.

We were fascinated by a country so different from England and readily took photographs to record what we were seeing. Colour-slide film was expensive then; I'd expected to cover the holiday with just three films of thirty-six exposures. I'd certainly wasted quite a few shots clicking from the train as we raced through the mountains and valleys of Austria, but it was all new, all worth capturing. Even so, it was worth a plaintive comment home: *I could use a whole colour film. As it is, I'm on the third of my films already and I've had to buy another.* Such extras ate holes in my limited budget.

At that moment a gust of hot wind caught the straw hat I'd bought in Athens and whirled it away into the water of the inner harbour.

"E fallen in the water,' Mike said in his best high-pitched Goon voice.

'Oh, hell,' I said. I'd have to replace it. I needed to protect myself from the sun even though my head of hair was bushy enough then. I watched the hat floating on the water like an upside down coracle. I couldn't see how it could be retrieved since it was some distance away in the water and sailing merrily along. I'd have to look for a place to buy another. But the wind which had tormented and teased me became my ally. It blew the hat gently towards the quay where we stood and, within a few minutes, I was able to clamber down some steps and pick it up. It was damp, of course, and smelt a little of the sea, but it would soon dry on my head. I kept that hat for more than twenty years

– a distinctly tangible souvenir of this holiday. I got rid of it only when the straw of the crown split and gaped at the sun.

Did we find a café on the harbour for our breakfast? Had we eaten on the boat? I cannot believe that we weren't hungry. Later that morning, we went to a very attractive wide beach where we bathed until lunchtime. The water was a beautiful dark blue. The wind had whipped up the waves and the sea looked as if it was pounding a Cornish surfing beach.

Already the sun beat down on us and I covered myself in sun-tan oil, but even so, I soon had to put my shirt on. I'd started to go quite pink after an hour. I was always chary of sunburn after a particularly unpleasant episode in the dunes of Dawlish Warren where I got badly burned, developed sunstroke and drivelled my way deliriously through the night.

Here, everything was new to us and worth recording:

The sand's incredibly hot, almost too hot to walk on, and we've attracted a crowd of Cretans, one of whom speaks English. The questions seem to be 'Deutsch? Americano? Ah, Inglis! Ha, Ha, Ha.'

Whether their laughter was relief is hard to tell. It seemed the Americans were not overly popular, and Germans, though tolerated, certainly were not.

It's just as well that we'd made some friends on that beach. While bathing from a beach which sloped away quickly in the water, Mike and John had the nasty experience of being caught in an undertow and couldn't get back to the beach. The backwash was so strong that they were being gradually drawn out to sea. Fortunately the crowd of young men on the beach saw what was happening and formed a human chain. They went into the water to the rescue and brought them back in. Both Mike and John looked shaken by their adventure and relieved to be back. John stood tall and silent on the beach, his hair plastered to his head. Mike, who rarely spoke much Modern Greek, rumbled an earnest *efharisto* and went round shaking hands. It was a lucky escape and a warning to us all.

Mike had other reasons to remember bad experiences while bathing. At some point he put his bare foot down on the sea bed and trod on a sea urchin. We'd been warned about them. If one of the spines breaks off and it penetrates the skin, it can inflict a painful wound. Mike was lucky; some Greeks realised what had happened and squeezed and pinched the underneath of his foot until the broken end of the spine could be seized and pulled out. It was like removing a very large splinter. Crisis over; but if he'd left it there, further problems could have occurred as it festered, and he might well have been hobbling painfully for some time. Folk remedies abounded, including using on an olive oil poultice. I found my own remedy; from then on I always wore my gym shoes in the sea so that I could put my foot down with impunity. At last I knew what sea creature Tatiana had been warning me about on the train – the one expression she couldn't translate: *morski jež* – sea urchin.

★ ★ ★

In the afternoon we returned to our Classical sight-seeing. About three miles out of Heraklion, we came to the ancient site of the Palace at *Cnossos*. The location was the stuff of legend, mentioned by Homer and supposedly the centre of power of Minos, King of Crete (possibly even *the* minos.)

Here was situated the mythical labyrinth with its dreaded inhabitant, the Minotaur, half-bull, half man. The old story was that you could easily get lost in the twists and windings of the tunnels. But fearful dark tales of our primary school days had yielded to the sunshine of our Classical learning.

We now knew that about 1600 years BC there had once been an early form of Greek civilization here, which became known as the Minoan civilization, and that it had developed its own language, some of which had been deciphered only in the preceding decade. We were visiting a place incredibly old and excitingly new. The civilisation was destroyed completely, possibly by a tsunami after a gigantic volcanic eruption underwater at the Island of Thera (now Santorini), some sixty-eight miles away. Word had it that the place was a halfway house from Egyptian civilization and showed elements of its influence. Now each of us, like a latterday Theseus, had come over from Athens to explore.

But the Cnossos we were to see was itself controversial. Sir Arthur Evans, who'd done the excavation work for the first thirty-five years of the twentieth century had believed in restoration in order to give an impression of the original appearance of the place. But purists shook their heads at the idea of setting in concrete the old ruins. I welcomed it. From the work he'd done I could envisage something of how the buildings might have looked. Here was a Classical site that wasn't just a pile of toppled stones. It had some life about it.

I recorded my pleasure in a letter: *I take back something of what I said. I've just looked over the ancient city of Cnossos – the oldest Greek civilisation known. Were they civilised! At least three storeys, and drainage, water supply and all ancient cons well laid on. This is about 1600 B.C. Some people think the King's Palace was the labyrinth, and it's not surprising. I've never come across such a complicated system of passages, steps, doorways and dead ends.*

The approach to the site was welcoming enough – spacious, ordered and uncluttered, and overlooked benignly by the bust of Sir Arthur Evans.

There is a Land Amid the Wine-Dark Sea

Immediately, the different levels and storeys of the building were evident. And more importantly we were entering a different world. Pillars, lintels and frescoes glowed with vitality and colour. At last!

Earlier in 1959, I'd appeared in The Cambridge Greek Play, *Antigone,* and the designer had taken Cnossos and Minoan civilization as his model for both the set and the costumes – another connection which brought the place alive for me, as I said to my parents on a picture postcard: *you can see now where the ideas for the Greek Play came from.*

You could believe that the palace itself had been a metaphor for the labyrinth. It extended over a large site and seemed incredibly complex. Apart from having three or four storeys, it was possible to see two doorways side by side and find that both of them led away to different parts of the building. Take a wrong turn and you could quickly get lost. The building had stairs, corridors, cellars, even seeming dead-ends.

None of us had seen Pompeii then, but here was a site sixteen hundred years older which showed all the signs of modern living. It was clear that the Minoans had running water, probably areas for ceremonial bathing (Evans called them lustral basins) and drainage, as did the Romans. But whereas the Romans had developed glass, this building had wide stairwells open to the sky to let in light and, no doubt in winter, cold as well.

We admired the brightly coloured pillars which appeared wider at the top than at

their base – unlike the Doric columns we'd seen in Athens – and they were painted a glorious terracotta red. Even one-time timber lintels had been reproduced in concrete and painted to give the impression of wood.

We wandered around, sometimes surprised that the route we'd taken brought us back to our starting point. The labyrinth was a place of wonder.

As well as bright pillars and walls, there were reproductions of some of the decorations the rooms once had. Most impressive, however, were the many painted frescoes depicting something of Minoan life. Both men and women had long hair.

At some instinctive level, we felt the influence of Egypt behind this civilization; maybe it was the men in skirts… But we could also see something of the coming Greek here.

There were too many frescoes for us to photograph everything. Scenes of nature were particularly eye-catching. No doubt some enterprising publisher has produced a glossy book capturing them all for tourists as overwhelmed as we were.

But the most significant fresco was one we knew from school days: the mysterious bull-leaping. Even now, not enough is known about the significance of these images. It's generally believed that the bull was considered sacred and worshipped. We're lurched back again to Theseus who had to face the challenge of the Minotaur. The fresco shows a young man somersaulting over the head of a charging bull. There are suggestions that the bull's head might actually toss him and help him on his way over. I still puzzle whether this picture is of three young men performing this extraordinary acrobatic feat or one man in different stages of the action. Did Theseus have to face some challenge like this with a Cretan bull?

There is a Land Amid the Wine-Dark Sea

We spent a long time wandering the site. Chris was particularly keen to record everything that was significant and memorable. Debate still continues about what Sir Arthur Evans called the Horns of Consecration. Were they symbolic representations of the horns of the sacred bull of Cnossos? Was it a ritual seat? Or were they used to 'capture' the sun at an important date in the year such as we know at Stonehenge, or even the War Memorial Arboretum at Alrewas?

Chris also photographed the *pithoi*, huge storage jars which had been reconstructed and positioned in some Minoan storage room. For my part, I looked at their size and shape and remembered the old story of Ali Baba and the Forty Thieves. Perhaps it was possible, after all, to conceal a man inside some of them. As a child I'd never believed it.

With characteristic understatement, Chris described Cnossos as *quite a place, partly restored.*

My particular obsessions also surfaced in a letter: *I've had to change into my long trousers – my legs are all red and glowing after this morning's exposure alone. I'm rubbing oils and lotions in… At the moment everybody's rubbing their sore legs. We're sitting in the shade of some pine trees – nearly deafened by the hundreds of chirping cicadas around.*

We managed to find, after some difficulty, a school in Heraklion which was left open as basic overnight accommodation for students. Others in our larger party, also in Crete, told us earlier in the day about the place, but didn't tell us where it was. Chris takes up the story: *When the time came for kip, we went to the Tourist Police, and of course they didn't know either. They said come back in half an hour and they'd have found out. We were sitting sipping a cognac when the chap who told us of the school went by. So we asked him where it was, got the key, told the tourist police we'd found it and off we went. Spent a very comfortable night, too, despite feet being rather sunburnt from morning's bathe. I'm glad I didn't leave my shirt off for long.*

And so to bed, mucking in, roughing it, complaining about the incompetence of Greeks – and tourist police in particular – but still managing to afford Greek brandy (κονιακ – koniak) after the end of our meal.

Monday August 10th:
Our plans were to go into the remote interior of Crete to see the other Minoan site, first discovered in late Victorian times but left largely unexcavated until the 1950s. Going to *Phaestos* would mean a bus journey across the island to the southern area, close to the Libyan Sea. It was not an established tourist route. We'd have to travel on the normal service bus.

All of us were tired that morning, feeling under the weather after the debilitating heat on the beach the previous day, but chores had to be done: we booked up for our return boat journey to Athens, and asked the tourist police for the time of the bus to Phaestos. Two o'clock we were told.

Then, what to do? Chris thought Mike and I were lazy when we opted to spend the morning writing; but he and I found some shady spot, perhaps even in the school itself, and stayed put. We probably also guarded all four rucksacks since, whenever possible, we avoided heaving our luggage onto our sunburnt backs. But Chris and John were energetic and went off for another bathe, undeterred by the scare of the previous day. We all met up at the school for lunch which we'd bought from various traders.

'I'm sure we were rooked,' John said when we considered the cost of our meagre lunchtime food.

'Come on, chaps, don't want to miss the bus.' Chris began tidying his rucksack, ready to leave.

'I hate rushing in this heat,' I said.

We stood at the appointed bus stop for an hour.

'Have we missed the bloody thing?' Mike eased his rucksack onto the ground.

We made enquiries and got reassurances that yes, the bus would be going soon. We waited patiently, trying to keep out of the sun.

'Two o'clock! That's what they said!' Chris was cross now. 'The tourist police are more hindrance than help. I don't know why we bother.'

'To-morrow, the bus he come to-morrow,' Mike said, in a cod foreign accent.

At last, the battered old single decker arrived. We clambered on board, bundling our luggage in front of us down the gangway. The heat beat down on the roof, and the other passengers looked at us with curiosity. It was going to be a long afternoon. The journey took us through spectacular scenery – the first time we'd really travelled through mountains apart from on the train. But it was hot, the scenery was parched brown and bare, and the road was not properly made up, little more than a cart track at times. For two and a quarter hours there was effectively nothing to do. We couldn't get up and wander around as we could on a ship or the train. To pass the time, two of us struck up a stumbling conversation with a fellow traveller – a girl – but both parties had to converse in halting French. I doubt we said anything memorable.

At last we arrived at the site of *Phaestos*. The bus stopped and dropped us off. Abandoned us almost. It was 5.15. PM

The sun was already slanting low and casting long shadows. We'd arrived at the site of the ruins; there was no village, only the tourist pavilion and the house of the archaeologist for the site. There was little time now to start exploring this more basic version of a Minoan palace.

'Perhaps we'd better go down and make ourselves known,' Chris said. 'Don't want to find they've shut up shop for the day.'

'I must have something to eat before kip.' John began striding down the track to the straggle of buildings. 'Aren't you starving?'

One by one we picked up our rucksacks and began to follow him. Chris, as always with an eye for a good photograph, began to take pictures.

'Pretty bare. What a God-forsaken place,' Mike said. He and I stood looking down at the valley in which Phaestos nestled.

That night has gone down in my memory as the most deprived of our holiday. When we asked at the tourist pavilion if we could have a meal, the man shrugged apologetically and said that he had nothing he could give us – except eggs and rice. That would have to do. He cooked our meal rapidly and then closed up the pavilion.

'I suppose we could kip on the roof,' John said. 'I don't fancy anywhere else.'

The man said that would be all right, and we began to move our stuff up there, clumping up the concrete steps of an outside staircase. The roof itself was surrounded by a low parapet, the whole building nestling up against the rampart of a hill at the back.

The man gave us a plate and spoon each, which we could give back in the morning when he returned, and we grumbled our way through eggs and rice while squatting on the roof.

'It'll be a wonder if we don't suffer from night starvation. What a place!' Poor old John, always thinking of his guts.

Chris busied himself and took a late photograph of Phaestos while it was largely empty.

We sat up in our eyrie, watching night creep into the valley. Because of the height and the isolation, we passed a cold night on that mountain plain.

★ ★ ★

Tuesday August 11^{*th*}

Tuesday August 11th

The next morning the valley bowl in which Phaestos was situated lay open to the sun and quickly became very hot. Grumblingly hungry after last night's snack, we made a listless tour of the palace, supposedly second only to Cnossos in grandeur. But here all was monochrome and mostly on one level. Modern archaeology, resumed less than a decade earlier, frowned on reconstruction, and so we were faced with an impression of a much flatter site and certainly none of the colour that Evans had used to bring Cnossos alive. The stone shone golden in the sun and was impressive enough. We wandered up the wide grand staircase and idled through various rooms whose walls were little more than waist-high. We were back with a traditional Classical site of low stone ruins and sawn-off pillars; to imagine what it was really like we'd have to look out an artist's impression of the palace. Here was no mysterious labyrinth. We ambled over to an area where a bright stretch of canvas sagged and lifted over the latest excavations. We ducked underneath and smelt the heat, the stone and the dust, all tinged with the hot green of the canvas-light. We burrowed there for the sake of completeness; what we saw meant little to us. Above us, the covering flapped in the light breeze.

'Shall we wander, lads?' John said. 'See if we can find some food.'

The tourist pavilion had no food for sale, much to our disgust, but we had a little of the previous night's rice and some salad left and made do with sharing that. A long time to wait for the bus to take us back to civilization. It left for Heraklion at 3 PM. We knew it departed from a nearby village and began a listless trek towards it. We wanted to be sure of a place. It was important we connected with the boat back to Athens which left at 7 PM. If the bus journey followed the same pattern as the day before, we'd be back in the harbour area at 5.15.

★ ★ ★

We all had different pastimes at slack moments like this. Both Mike and John liked to sketch. I often spent time catching up with my diary and trying to record details for such time as I would write up this account. I didn't envisage then that it would take fifty years before I began work on the project. Some things I recorded in the diary had just one word, either through pressure of time or because the event was searingly obvious and memorable. A one-word prompt was all I needed.

Or so I thought.

In places, it is difficult to recreate what happened; in others I'm still able to watch an old, grainy film in my mind and bring those far-off days to life again.

Chris was busy writing a long letter home that afternoon and was keen to talk about food and drink – an obvious subject that hungry day.

His youthful enthusiasm shines through. *Food: most of the time it's pretty good. It's never more expensive than at home, tho' it's dearer in Athens than elsewhere. We've found a jolly good restaurant in Athens and have had some marvellous dishes, with various wines. Melons, water- and yellow variety, are delicious and go with nearly every meal. All drinks are served ice-cold, and ice-cold clear water comes free with everything. It's marvellous stuff. I didn't know water could taste so good. The best wine we've had is here in Crete – 1/6 or 2/-a bottle. It's white and delicious. We very often end a meal with a brandy or a liqueur of some sort (esp. Benedictine for me) which costs 1/- or 9d – about twice as much [in the glass] as you get at home. A dish of pipless little grapes is delicious, a moussaka is gorgeous (a glorified cottage pie, only beautifully spiced). Ice creams in the streets are huge cornet-fulls for 4d, deliciously creamy. Beer is cheap per glass, but by bottle it's more expensive, tho' no more than an equal amount of lager in England. Had a beautiful one this morning – ice-cold, tasting like nectar. It's hotter here than in mainland Greece, and beer is luvly!*

There was hardly a proper bus stop in that hot, anonymous village near Phaestos. The battered vehicle, its paintwork dented and scarred as if from bullets or stones, stood right in the middle of the road, waiting for passengers. The heat beat down. The driver had flung the door open, and many of the sliding passenger windows had been yanked down to let in air. Having bagged our places on the bus, we came out again, hanging about, waiting for departure. As far as we could see, there were very few other motor vehicles there – an old Citroen, perhaps. Certainly none of the flash American limousines that glided around Athens. Much of the transport was by hand-cart or one pulled by a donkey.

There is a Land Amid the Wine-Dark Sea

An old woman had positioned herself in the deep shade of a large olive tree, her trays of apples set out on a little trundle cart. It seemed a good idea to buy something for the journey. With luck, we'd eat in Heraklion before the voyage. Nearby, a small boy with a tray slung around his neck waited hopefully for some traveller to buy a few of his sweetmeats. Apart from taking his photograph, we ignored him. His hair cropped close presumably to reduce the risk of nits, he smiled anxiously at us, uncertain whether to press us to buy his offerings.

Much of the luggage was carried on the roof of the bus. Mysterious parcels, sack-covered, were already lashed down. I was shocked when, shortly before departure, a woman bustled up, carrying a writhing sack. She handed this to the driver who was standing near the bus. He drew out a brown chicken and held it upside down. The bird began to flap and squawk.

Holding the chicken by its legs, he passed it up to another man on the roof who lashed its feet to the low barrier rail.

I heard the thump of footsteps above and hated the way the bird hung flapping and squawking at the side of the bus. Its eye seemed to glare accusingly. The beak gaped. A companion hen joined it upside down at the window. We were almost ready to depart.

I watched a feather float to the floor and wondered how the hens would survive the journey. Perhaps they wouldn't…

Chris turned to me and muttered: 'Rural Crete for you.' He had continued to write his long letter, grouping his subjects into categories. I smile now at the words of a future banker: *Money: on the whole seems to be going on travelling. We've done quite a bit, and have paid for last*

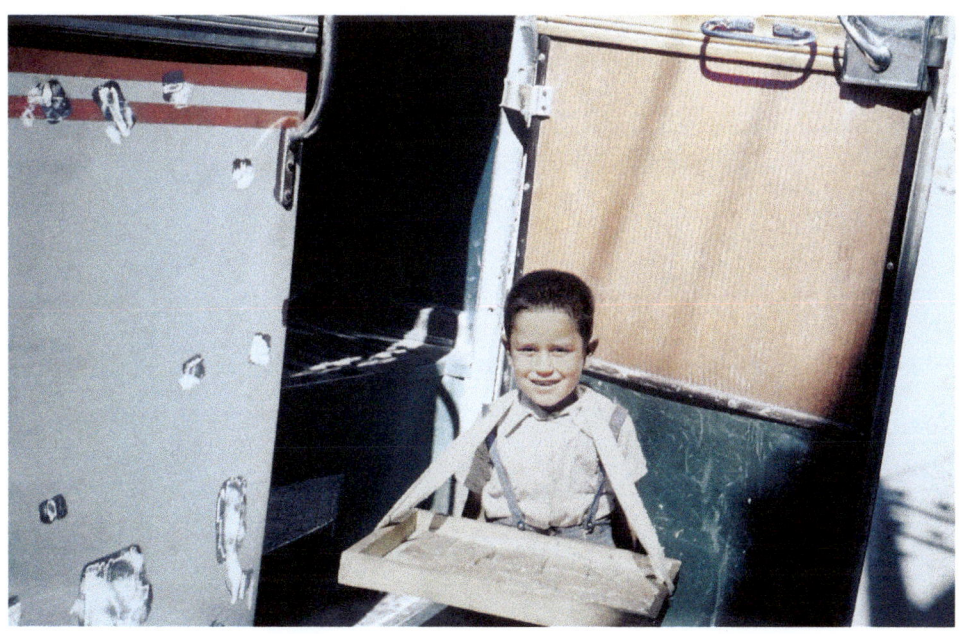

week already. Also we're spending quite a bit on food and will probably have to cut down. I'll last out easily enough, but Richard is cutting his finances a bit fine. He had a £45 travel grant, too, and worked for 4 weeks at £9 a week. He's a bit of a fool moneywise.

Again, after a ride in the bus of nearly three hours, we were back in Heraklion and began to think about catching the boat back to Athens. No doubt we had an early meal and Chris had his beer; then onto the boat for the return trip. But things were different this time. They had herded a load of cattle onto the ship, presumably for slaughter on the mainland. It wasn't just the smell of the sea we had to cope with that night.

On our arrival in Crete, I very nearly lost my hat in the harbour; on our departure, Mike managed to lose his sunglasses somewhere – a fact which unsettled him. He spent some time checking his baggage and trying to work out how and where he'd mislaid them, the most likely explanation being that they had slipped out of the breast pocket of his shirt.

The other factor that made the journey North different was that we had a strong wind blowing across the ship. For once we were almost cold. The voyage was hardly memorable; we didn't bother with the dawn. We'd seen it all before.

At some point, Chris did manage to get a picture of a windswept me up in the bows of the ship.

★ ★ ★

Wednesday August 12th

After another twelve-hour crossing, it became increasingly obvious we'd arrive back in *Piraeus* later than expected. Perhaps the head wind had slowed us. Nevertheless, people on the boat began their daily routine, making sure they were ready for arrival in Athens.

Such early morning preparations as shaving were not necessary for us; we continued to let our beards grow.

As a group we all got on well but often broke up into pairs: Chris with John, Mike with me. He and I had become easy-going friends soon after arriving at King's, comfortable enough to call each other 'mate' almost from the start. This may well have been a nod towards *The Goon Show* which we'd both listened to avidly as teenagers. But something was niggling Mike this morning: he'd lost his sunglasses; perhaps he hadn't slept well on deck; maybe being surrounded by Greek chatter had finally got to him, or, quite possibly, I made some crass remark which sparked him off. I've never forgotten my shock at the tirade of anger which he let loose as we slipped into the harbour at Piraeus. It seemed directed at me. I came from a family where we sat on

our anger. I felt bewildered at the torrent of furious words that flowed around me, and withdrew into a hurt silence. Mike apologised later, of course, and soon he was back to fooling about and we were 'mating' again.

We knew we wanted to visit the Greek Islands. There's some suggestion that we hoped to set off the same day for Rhodes. That didn't happen because of our late arrival, so we had time to kill, and plans to re-arrange. It seems our fear of being rooked surfaced again over our breakfast. Bloody Greeks! Hungry after all that sea air, we felt we'd not had much to eat for the price we paid.

Time to head back to the centre of Athens; again we took the metro to Omonia Square and began visiting our old haunts; we called in on the Lux hotel and exchanged some of our clothes; all of us made a point of going to Cooks where the *Poste Restante* offered our one link with home. Mike was particularly anxious for some mail. Would his driving licence have arrived?

Chris's needs were more mundane. He wanted his folks to send out another shirt. We must all have attempted wash-basin laundry from time to time with varying degrees of success. Chris recorded his situation: *I've washed one or two times – the rayon shirt with red squares is crumpled beyond recognition, and after rough handling in a sink there are several holes appearing. That goes too, for the red and black, and red and blue shirts but they're not crumpled. Underpants and socks wash OK. Handkerchiefs dicy, don't wear a vest.* Though we had been advised to take nylon shirts with us, drip-dry shirts were a comparatively new phenomenon and probably not in our luggage.

We planned to set off for the *Greek Islands* almost straight away, so we spent some time stocking up with food to take with us. We had, of course, to return to Piraeus to catch the boat. Our intention was to catch the SS *Pantelis*, but for reasons we didn't understand at the time the boat was full. My notes record an alarming encounter with a mad woman but nothing more. One of those one-word prompts. Things weren't going our way. Now we had the rest of the day to fill. To ensure a place, we made a firm booking on Thursday's boat and decided to find something else to do. No point in checking into the Lux hotel just for one night. We'd save money and find somewhere a little outside the city to camp. We headed again for the metro out of Piraeus and took the train to *New Phaleron* – an area not too far away which offered seaside and a beach. There we ate some of our stock of food for lunch.

Any idea of spending an afternoon bathing in the sea had to be quickly abandoned. The smell of sewage made it obvious that it wasn't appropriate. We drifted further along the coast until we came to a small seaside place called *Edem*. It wasn't attractive, but it would have to do. Later that day, while drinking a beer, we were buttonholed by a chap who could speak English. He talked at length to us and was at pains to warn us about bandits, as he called them. We were obviously in an area where thieves wouldn't hesitate to lift our possessions if we weren't careful.

We don't know if he was an elaborate con artist or skillfully distracting us for an accomplice. At some point, Mike's camera disappeared. Whether he mislaid it or it was stolen we never knew. He was very put out about the loss because he had to rely even more on his sketching in order to record our holiday. He'd already been niggled that Chris had called the camera cheap and old when its shutter jammed on Crete. As darkness closed in, we began to prepare for our night outside. We'd sleep on the beach, the sand was soft and dry and it'd make a comfortable place to kip. Unfortunately we were still too close to civilisation. People chattered and laughed at a nearby night club, and the juke-box kept us awake until 2.30 am. One tune in particular, *Mantoumpala*, loud and wailing in the darkness, was belted out several times that night and became a theme tune for the holiday. Clearly a hit of the time.

★ ★ ★

Thursday August 13th

We woke up late, feeling the sun hot on us and found that our sandy beach was not only soft and dry but much dirtier than we thought. Cigarette ends and other debris surrounded us, but the most disturbing factor was that it was home to huge ants – about an inch across, we reckoned. Long spindly creatures, like aggressive daddy longlegs, they scurried about everywhere. I alone, raised on my lilo, had not been bitten; the others checked and found that the ants had made free and got inside their sleeping bags as they sank into the sand. That occurrence must have decided us to follow advice and surround ourselves with a ring of ant powder if we slept directly on the ground again.

We breakfasted on chunky bread. I'd bought an interesting tube of marmalade on our foraging, not unlike a toothpaste tube, which we each used, taking a squeeze of the sticky jam onto the bread to make it more palatable. Inside the carton which contained it, I found a yellow slip of paper which promoted the product and promised to give us *'healt'*. I kept that paper for years, obviously amused at the solecisms the translation produced. Like so many continental products, it was not a taste of home or anything like marmalade as we knew it.

We split up after breakfast: Mike set off again for central Athens, still keen to see if the little red-book driving licence had arrived in the post. We undertook to see if we could investigate further what had happened to his camera, and began a slow wander back towards Edem.

We were appalled to see in the bright daylight how much sewage there was on the beach. The oppressive smell hung on the air.

'Wouldn't fancy a dip here, lads,' John said.

Chris and I agreed, and we drifted on. But soon afterwards we saw something which shocked me, but also spoke volumes about the poverty of some Greeks at that time. We came across an area where old women were standing on the beach half-clothed and rubbing themselves all over with dry sand. They scooped up great handfuls and used it like pumice to freshen their skin. It made sense; perhaps they also used olive oil, and we were witnessing a sort-of throwback to the days of the strigil scraper. They were quite unselfconscious: they lumbered and waddled, quite ungainly as they changed out of their underclothes, but they took no notice of us. Like good British boys, we looked away, so I cannot now say whether they made use of the sea to wash the sand off. We were witnessing life at a level even lower than the Lux hotel offered. We couldn't record it in a photograph, but the image remains firm in my memory. Only later did Chris manage a picture that showed how common it was for the sea to be a place for bathing and cleansing.

The separation of the classes was even more apparent further along that sea-front. All the best beaches had been fenced off and taken over for hired bathing. Old Phaleron, further on past Edem, was clearly the rich quarter. Small palm trees adorned the front, and it was altogether a more inviting place, though whether back-packing students would have gained admission is open to question.

John, often impatient at our progress, strode on ahead while Chris and I continued at a more leisurely pace. After about three quarters of an hour, we approached a man who seemed an important dignitary but who incongruously wore no more than a hat and bathing trunks. We asked him about Mike's camera and what we should do. There'd been no sign of it, and his suggestion was that we should go on further round the bay of Phaleron and make enquiries at the police station at *Flisvos*.

Mid-morning now and the three of us opted to have a drink in a café. No sight-seeing, not much to do. Still worried about Mike's camera, I wandered hopefully into the café next door in the hope that the camera had been handed in. But welcoming though they were, no one spoke English; the only chance of communication was with a boy waiter who spoke German badly. Under the stress of the moment, my schoolboy German vanished, and I realised I didn't know the German for 'lost': *verloren*. Nothing for it but to use what little skill I had at miming. But I found it very difficult to get the concept across. I took my own camera from around my neck, put it on the floor and walked away. All the Greeks in the café looked at me as if I was mad. The ploy was clearly no use. I finally managed to solve the problem by involving a man ensconced in a kiosk outside the café. He at least understood some French; I must have known the verb for to lose, and the man explained in Greek what I wanted to say to the boy waiter who'd watched all my antics with increasing curiosity. At last the boy understood what the problem was. He looked directly at me, rolled his head in a slight upward Greek nod and said: *Nein!*

We were beginning to run out of options. We should hurry on and see if we could find the police station, as the stout dignitary had suggested. But again nobody spoke English, not even the big fat commissioner, as I called him. Once more Greek ingenuity came to the fore and translation was achieved through the barber next door who paused in the middle of his work to explain our problem to the police. He had, of course, to translate their response back to us. Meanwhile the customer in the chair became increasingly irate at being ignored and left half shorn.

Our new destination was to be No 6 Poseidon Road, the headquarters of the Navy beach patrol. It was logical; if Mike had lost the camera on the beach, it could have been handed in there for safe-keeping. But something got lost in the translation. When we found that particular address, it turned out to be a private house full of women. I waited at the foot of the stairs up to the front door, while the women clustered at the doorway laughing at Chris' and John's predicament. What did the women think the two wanted? Had we made the mistake, or had we all been directed to a brothel? Somewhere we could take dirty photographs, perhaps…

Eventually we found the Navy headquarters but pessimism was beginning to set in.

'I think it's unlikely they can help,' Chris said. 'What would the Navy want with a tourist camera? Shall we leave it?'

'I agree,' John began a fast walk back to where we'd agreed to meet Mike. 'It's getting late; I'm starving.'

We found a workman's café where we could have lunch cheaply.

'Sorry, Splot,' John said, when Mike joined us. 'We tried, but no luck.'

Mike rumbled his thanks, obviously disappointed at having no camera for the rest of the holiday. It was impractical to think of buying one, and none of us would want to lend him shutter-time with our cameras.

The café was proud of its American juke box. The sound didn't seem half as pervasive and noisy as the previous night. Greeks wandered into the café, bought something to eat or drink and fed money into the machine. Again, we heard several times the one tune *Mantoumpala* which had wailed through our troubled sleep the previous night.

Curiosity made us look round the café. It seemed much better equipped than those we knew at home. Most places we went into in Greece seemed to have vast fridges installed – a necessity, presumably, in that summer heat.

'It'd be interesting to see what a high-class restaurant would be like,' I said, 'if ordinary cafés have this sort of equipment.'

We all agreed, but restlessness was in the air. We paid our dues, shouldered our rucksacks and headed for the bus stop to wait for a bus to Piraeus. Time to think about the Greek Islands.

No One Knows Nothing on this Mad Ship

'Where you boys going?' The taxi drew up alongside as we waited patiently at the bus stop.

'Piraeus,' I called. 'Catch a boat.'

'OK,' the driver replied, 'ten drachmas.'

'Shall we?' John wrinkled his face in distrust.

'Ten drachmas. I take you to Piraeus.'

'All of us and our baggage? You take our luggage as well?' Mike eased his rucksack off his shoulder.

'I take everything. Ten drachmas.'

'Better not be a catch,' said Chris as we piled three of the bags into the boot.

John, the tallest, sat in the front with his bag on his knee. 'Cross your fingers, lads.' He straightened his black beret and grinned at the three of us in the back.

We recognised none of the roads as the speeding taxi weaved through the Athens traffic. Even the Acropolis seemed to be on the wrong side.

'I think it's the right direction,' Chris murmured in my ear. 'Judging by the sun.'

Soon the car was down on the waterfront, juddering over cobbles.

'What called your boat?' the driver said, over his shoulder.

'Despina,' Chris said, using the modern Greek pronunciation.

'OK, I take you. You going Greek Islands?'

The taxi drew up alongside a ship and stopped.

'This is it!' said John.

We eased ourselves out and began lifting our baggage onto the quay.

'What do you think?' said Chris. He had the ten drachmas ready in his hand.

'Let's make it twelve,' said Mike, 'I reckon it's worth it, bringing us right here.'

So, without haggling, we happily paid the driver twelve drachmas, thanked him and slammed the car doors.

'There she is: *Despoina*.' I used our ancient Greek pronunciation. '*Mistress*.'

'Looks pretty bloody crowded,' Mike said as we clambered aboard, trying not to hit people with our rucksacks. We swung round tight corners and clambered up a narrow staircase towards the deck.

'Shall we head up front again, lads?' John strode ahead.

But we were out of luck. The bow area was already crowded with passengers who'd obviously been settled there for some time.

'Who are all these people?' I said.

We learned quickly enough that we were on a pilgrim boat heading not only for Mykonos, but stopping first at the Greek islands of Syros and Tinos. In a letter home Chris later described the scene: *the ship full of cripples, madmen, and idle peasants who ought to be flogged, all going to Tinos to this wretched festival – Roman Catholics all, madmen!*

Ah, the Englishman abroad…

Most passengers were pilgrims going to the shrine of the Madonna on Tinos. Apparently, it's the Greek Orthodox church's most sacred island with the famous monastery of the Madonna, whom pilgrims from all over Greece honour on the 15th of August – the day of The Assumption. They flock there in the hope of a glimpse of the icon, or to receive some token of its miraculous powers for curing the sick and helping those suffering misfortune.

We'd chosen to travel two days before the major festival. Whichever boat we caught would be packed like this. The ship's company had made some effort to protect the many passengers from the heat of the sun. They'd slung a huge tarpaulin up over part of the deck to act as shelter; already several crammed beneath its hot shade. Other peasants improvised their own, tying up blankets to various parts of the ship in order to afford some protection against the sun's rays. Others sat where they could.

We managed to find space for ourselves against the starboard side of the ship on the metal part of the deck. Only when we tried to sit down did we discover why no one else had taken the place. The deck was burning hot and offered absolutely no shelter from the sun.

'Is this a good idea?' I asked, always concerned about getting sunburnt.

'Not much choice,' Mike said, 'there's still an hour to go before sailing. And the buggers are still coming on board.'

We decided to make the best of it and spread a groundsheet as insulation against the hot metal deck, and sat on it, leaning against our rucksacks. Not very effective, but this would have to be our patch until we reached Mykonos in the late evening.

The boat continued to fill up so that there was scarcely room to move. As the ship prepared to sail, people perched on the hawser and even on the bows of the ship.

At last, at two o'clock, Despoina slipped away from the quay and began the slow glide out of Piraeus. A light breeze sprang up.

'Hullo, boys! How are you?' We smiled a response; we were used to this. A small, dapper, middle-aged Greek stood by my side, looking up at me. He must have been in his late forties.

'German?'

'No, English.'

When he began talking it soon became evident he was more cultured and better educated than many other Greeks we'd met. He began pointing out distant landmarks. 'You know the Acropolis, of course. The pride of Athens. It's very old.'

'Yes, I know,' I said. 'We've already been there. Three of us are students of Classics – Ancient Greek and Latin.'

'Ah, you are educated, so you know. Here in Greece many poor people. In Piraeus live many poor people. Not a nice place to live. Crowded, dirty. Over there,' he pointed out a broad bay fading into the distance, 'is Old Phaleron. Very nice place. Big houses, space. The rich people of Athens live Old Phaleron. Much poverty, much ignorance in Greece. See all these folcks here?' He waved an arm. 'Peasants. Stupid people.' He knew the word *folk*, not how to pronounce it.

'Richard, sorry to interrupt. I thought you might want to see the dolphins.' Chris already had his camera out.

'Excuse me,' I said, and left the stranger.

Chris directed me to a small space where I could look over the side, near the bows. Amidst the glitter and spray of the water, dolphins leapt and plunged just in front of the boat's surge, so close you'd think the bows would slice their bodies. I reached for my camera and leaned over the side as far as I dared. The creatures were clearly visible just below the surface. From time to time they arced out of the water, their snouts seeming to smile for my camera.

'Extraordinary sight,' I said to Chris. 'Amazing they don't get hurt.'

'Pretty intelligent. They're in no danger.'

I leaned again over the side and watched as, one by one, the dolphins leaped off sharply at a right angle to our course and disappeared.

'Marvellous. Thanks, Chris.'

I turned away and went back to join the others. But the mysterious stranger still hovered. I took a closer look at him: puffy rounded cheeks on a sensuous face, a strangely unpleasant, almost sinister mouth. His eyes darted everywhere, and he often rolled them as if trying to flirt and attract us. Most of his attention seemed to be directed towards me.

'So, you are student. Where do you make your studies?'

I told him Cambridge.

'I work as choreographer to the Athens State Ballet. I am very well known and have many successes in Europe: Berlin, Vienna, London. Your city London I know well. I have been many times – Piccadilly, Leicester Square, Soho.'

All the red light areas, I thought.

I'd already decided he was a bit of a bighead; he showed none of the modesty characteristic of an Englishman, and I judged him typical of the continent – lacking in inhibition and humility.

'My name is Angelos Grymanis. Perhaps you have heard of me.'

I could hardly say no, but I felt obliged to introduce myself.

After that he became more talkative and unnerved me as he seemed also to become more affectionate.

'You know, Reechard, you could become ballet dancer.' He ran his hand down my arm from the shoulder. 'You have fine figure. You come to me and I train you.'

'Oh, no. I couldn't do that. I'm too clumsy.'

'Clumsy? What is clumsy?'

I explained.

'Oh, no, that is not right. I teach you how to move.'

I thought it better to drop the subject and fell silent. I gave Mike a significant look indicating that I thought Angelo – as we came to call him – was rather odd. A Swiss couple who stood near our group intercepted that look and laughed. I assumed then that they laughed at Angelo's strange behaviour. But now…

The word *gay* was not in use then but I'd had some experience of the scene, after my part earlier in the year in the Cambridge Greek Play. There I encountered the composer, Peter Tranchell and the stage designer, Dr Malcolm Burgess who were obviously more than good friends. I was still dining out on stories about what I called the *queer* party I'd attended at the end of the play's run which Peter and Malcky had organised.

But all homosexual activities were still kept strictly underground in society as they were illegal, and our knowledge and acceptance of them was limited to gossip, hearsay and stereotyping. As Angelo was a male ballet trainer and one-time dancer, and as he used scent, as Malcolm Burgess did, I began to wonder about him. I certainly didn't understand about predators.

'Reechard, are you thirsty? Let me buy you drink.'

None of the others wished to be involved, so I went off alone with Angelo.

The boat was crowded with pilgrims and tourists and we had difficulty reaching the stern where the bar was. Angelo tried to get into the First Class bar instead, but was refused entry. A rapid exchange of Greek ensued.

'Reechard, the steward here recognises me, he knows who I am, of course. But he says he's very sorry he cannot let me in without the captain's permission. These stupid people and their rules.'

We set off to walk aft, weaving amongst those standing and lying on the deck. Many of the pilgrims slept in the heat, and small children curled up wherever there was space. We passed a woman dressed in black who looked as though she'd suffered a gunshot wound. She had only the remnants of a nose, one eye was covered with a bandage and her remaining bloodshot eye stared at us as we pushed past. It would take a miracle from the Madonna to heal her wounds.

Finally we managed to reach the bar and Angelo jostled his way forward. I declined anything alcoholic; in that heat, I needed something cool and refreshing.

'Here you are, Reechard. For you.' He handed me a lemonade and some sandwiches. 'All these folcks, these pilgrims, they are stupid. That old woman, at the bar, she says she is a hundred, ten years old. And that woman there–' He pointed to someone swathed in flowing clothes and holding a candle. 'That *washerwoman* – she is mad. Quite mad.'

A young soldier in uniform stood nearby, drinking a beer. Angelo spoke to him rapidly in Greek, and the young man smiled, then laughed. Angelo's response was to reach up and stroke the soldier's cheek with the back of his hand, then he clasped his arm affectionately.

He turned back to me: 'Reechard, Reechard...' His voice little more than an erotic whisper. 'When we get to Syros, and Tinos also, I will take you for walks on the island.'

'When will that be? When will we get there?' Already the journey seemed to be dragging.

'No one knows. No one knows nothing on this mad ship. But I am happy. I have company of Reechard.'

I decided to make use of Angelo's local knowledge: 'Do you know where the toilet is, Angelo?'

'You must go through that doorway and somewhere you see a door with the three circles.' He drew the shape on the palm of his hand. 'That is the toilet.'

'Ah, yes, I've come across that before. Thank you.'

'I wait here for you, Reechard.' He rolled his eyes at me.

★ ★ ★

We reached Syros about 8 PM and I told Angelo we must have food. Already I'd begun to think it wiser to keep him near Mike and the others. Immediately he offered to treat us all, sweeping us along with insistent generosity.

'Look, we'll stay here and keep these places,' Chris said.

'Something filling,' John said. 'I'm starving.'

Disembarkation took place at the stern of the boat. Mike and I followed Angelo into the vast crush of people shuffling towards the exit. In the end, we had only ten minutes to buy food and get back on board. But Angelo saw no need for urgency: he stopped first to buy loukoumia, seemingly unaware how we had responsibility to get food for the others.

'I will find nice restaurant for a meal where we can sit down, relax…'

'Angelo,' I insisted, 'there won't be time. Isn't there somewhere where we can buy food to take back onto the boat?'

'Oh, you don't want that. You want good food…'

'What about there?' I spotted a restaurant which didn't look busy.

We dashed in amongst the diners, Angelo making a great flourish as we entered. A rapid exchange of greetings in Greek. Handshakes all round.

'They know me here,' he explained.

Mike and I stood back, anxious about the time. On the counter in front of us we looked at fried squid on a plate.

'Not sure I fancy that,' Mike murmured.

But Angelo got the point and was now busy persuading the restaurant to give us some food to take away. The cooks put two portions of Makaronia Neapolitana (meat and spaghetti) into some paper, and then added cold potatoes, and bread and cheese – enough for us all. Quickly he took out his wallet and paid for everything. We carried all the food back to the ship in a cardboard box.

Five of us, including Angelo, each with one implement, began dipping into the paper which was spread out on a rucksack as a makeshift table.

In the semi-darkness, as the ship began ploughing out to sea again, we knelt, we squatted, we sat, we stood up, tucking into the hotch-potch of food: the craziest meal ever.

Angelo, despite his earlier disdain, showed tremendous enthusiasm for this 'picnic'. When we'd all eaten as much as we could manage, he produced the box of Greek Delight and we rounded off the meal with sweet-scented powdery jelly.

'That was very pleasant. Now, how much do we owe you?' Chris had his wallet ready.

'No, no, no. You pay nothing. It is my pleasure. When I am in London I stay YMCA. Today it is my turn to be hospitable. I am pleased to entertain four nice English boys.' With a final flourish he presented us with the remainder of the box of sweets.

'Oh, thank you very much.'

Chris and John, however, made it fairly plain they weren't happy with his constant presence. They found his generosity and his enthusiastic involvement with us overpowering. John beckoned me over and muttered out of the side of his mouth, 'Can't you do something? See if you can get rid of him!'

'Angelo,' I said, taking the hint, 'can we return your hospitality? Will you let us buy you a drink?' I made to move away towards the bar, and Angelo began to follow me. Mike, sensing I might need reinforcements, came too.

Angelo was a strange mixture. We found him an extremely good actor and mimic. Good company when he wasn't trying to impress. And he laughed a lot. Sometimes, though, he became very wearing. Some of his bizarre behaviour reminded me of the gay don at King's, Norman Routledge. But the word *camp* wasn't common parlance then. It's easy to say with hindsight I should have known what we were dealing with, but we didn't. Not then. We didn't know that Routledge was gay, either. We had our suspicions about his orientation, but no more.

I actually challenged him once when he took me out for a day trip in his Riley to see the churches of Norfolk: 'Norman, are you a homosexual?'

There was a pause. He didn't look at me. 'There are certain things, Wichard, you should never ask anyone.'

I apologised immediately, and no more was said. But that moment told him all he needed to know about me.

As Angelo, Mike and I pushed through the crowds on the way to the bar, I was surprised to see how such a sophisticated man was frightened by the gurning and jabber of a harmless lunatic bound for Tinos. Earlier, too, when we saw a Russian ship, he became agitated and afraid. We British took all these strange sights in our stride.

Angelo could not hide his relief when we reached Tinos. The boat at last began to empty. From the port side rail, we watched the stream of pilgrims flow off the ship and mingle with others on the quayside. Very crowded. This time Angelo made no suggestion of going for a walk on shore.

The boat didn't stop long and we were soon gliding out past bobbing lights on local fishing boats. High on the hillside, the Church of the Madonna, illuminated and welcoming, drew the eye. We turned back to our drink, anxious ourselves now for journey's end.

But I still had one task before we reached Mykonos.

Angelo was still with us as Mike and I returned from our drink. Specks of light ahead showed the boat was approaching the harbour of Mykonos.

'Angelo,' I said, 'when we get off the boat, the four of us will be going together to find somewhere to sleep. So I'll say goodbye now.'

I held out my hand and thanked him for his company and his generosity.

He took the hint very quickly and moved away, turning back only briefly to say, 'I shall see you again, Reechard.' It sounded almost sinister. Then he vanished into the crowd thronging the gangway.

I felt guilty and wondered afterwards whether he was lonely and thought he'd made a real friend in me. I felt a bit of a swine for some time.

★ ★ ★

Mykonos harbour was not deep enough for the boat to go right in, and so we were taken ashore by little motor boats. Even at 11.30 at night, I noticed that the sea was wonderfully clear as we'd been told to expect. As we neared the quay, I saw a French woman trying to explain to a Greek official that her bag was too heavy. She spoke her own language and he, not understanding, merely shrugged. Fortunately, my schoolboy French was up to scratch. I picked up her case and staggered down the plank carrying my rucksack and her luggage. She thanked me effusively – all of which I understood – and complimented me on my French.

'*Rien du tout, madame,*' I murmured and waited for the others. I discovered later, on the claustrophobic setting of that island, that the lady was an artist and also unmarried. I worried for some time whether I'd committed a grammatical *faux pas* by calling her *madame*.

We gathered on the quayside and thought about having a meal before finding somewhere to sleep.

'Not me, lads. Just ready for my kip.' John not hungry? That was a first.

The streets of Mykonos were small, twisty and impenetrable. Difficult to keep a clear direction in mind. It seemed we'd landed into a nightmare as we trudged through unending, dimly lit passages. We met no one and seemed to be going nowhere. Only hostile white walls stared at us, and steps leading up to tightly closed doors. The people of Mykonos had gone to bed. Only the restaurants waited for tourists.

Eventually we found sandy ground near some windmills. This would do. We were all very tired and began preparing to get into our sleeping bags. Looking up, I spotted a dim shape in the moonlight – a donkey – fortunately tethered.

We'd all dropped off when Chris woke to sounds of the animal walking closer. He sat up suddenly and must have startled the beast. It gave a noisy see-saw bray which echoed around the quiet of the island. We all woke up. From a far-off hillside came an answering donkey cry.

'Bloody hell,' Mike said. He yawned.

Chris, determined to have some safety from marauding animals, got out of his sleeping bag, moved all his bedding right round to the other side of the group and surrounded himself a second time that night with a fairy ring of DDT.

Games and Sordid Shouting Matches

Friday 14th August
We decided to relax on Mykonos – a break from the race round the 'musts' of the classical sites. Even so, we planned to visit the nearby island of Delos at some time.

Despite our determination to take it easy, we were woken early by chickens, more donkeys, and lorries. We'd spent the night in a farmyard. The ground was sandy, dusty, and hens scratched about nearby. We'd camped on the site of the iconic symbols of Mykonos – the windmills. There'd once been four or five on the slope of this hillside; now only one looked in working order. The others were in poor repair or piles of rubble. Breakfast was straightforward: we bought several rolls from itinerant sellers taking baskets of bread to the various scattered cottages on the island.

Our simple meal quickly filled us; we packed up and trudged back down to the quayside for a drink. The social centre of the island seemed to be the harbour area where all the main cafés and restaurants were situated.

We returned to our café of the previous night and found half of the original main party already there: Valerie Kesterton and Ann Brazier, Stephen Duckworth, another Kingsman, and others all rounding off their time on Mykonos. They'd obviously stayed elsewhere. We spent a few minutes exchanging greetings and news.

John and I slipped off to the local public lavatory – very basic facilities in white-washed stone, disturbingly close to the sea. There I had an argument with an elderly one-armed attendant who wanted to charge one drachma (3d) for the use of the toilet paper. I thought this price for spending a penny exorbitant and offered him 10 leptas instead. I'd seen several of these coins the night before in the little tray on the attendant's table. But he, offended, rejected my offer and shouted and gestured as if I'd insulted him. The whole thing developed into a sordid shouting match in our separate languages. Neither of us understood a word the other was saying. My solution was to borrow John's toilet paper and, ignoring the attendant, take possession of the throne.

Had he known, though, the man would have had the last laugh: I went away constipated.

On the way down to the quay, we bought some grapes from a seller, and like good

Englishmen, wanted them washed before we'd eat them. We couldn't see a public tap anywhere so we asked the café where we sat if they'd wash them for us and fill our water bottles. The response was very grudging; a surly waiter returned the grapes to us barely wet and handed over half-filled bottles. So much for our day's water supply.

'Mean bugger,' Mike said. 'Don't they want tourists to come to this island?'

'Yes, but perhaps they wanted us to buy the grapes from them.' Chris, always calm, seemingly the reasonable one, saw the other point of view.

'But we did have four Nescafés from them,' I added.

We chuntered on, walking back up the hill, past the windmills, for our day on the beach.

★ ★ ★

Seen from the long road sloping down to it, the sea was a beautiful turquoise – an effect emphasised by the light-coloured sand below the surface.

The beach had very few occupants, and we undressed quickly and plunged into the sea. It was the clearest water I have ever seen and splendidly warm. I began blowing up my blue lilo, taking care not to get giddy, put the bung in and cautiously floated it just in front of me. Then, lunging face down onto it, I paddled away from the shore. At first I saw spongy rocks below, possibly dangerous. About twenty yards out, we found a strip of sand in deep water and here we stayed as the safest place for a swim. No hidden hazards; we could see straight to the bottom. In one place I could stand with the water just up to my chin. I bobbed up and down on my toes, the warm water tickling and lapping my mouth. We took it in turns having a go on the lilo which floated serenely on the clear water. A good time for attacks and counter-attacks against the rider. Much splashing, shouting and laughter. We played and tumbled each other into the clear water, enjoying all the freedom and warmth of the Aegean Sea.

We spent the whole day on the beach, had an improvised lunch of grapes, peaches and chocolate, then lay down on the rough sand. Time to catch up on lost sleep. The sun blazed down from a clear sky, so we covered our bodies as much as possible. I put my shirt on and carefully spread my large bathing towel over my legs. Underneath I still wore my swimming trunks. Then I lay down, tilted my straw hat forward over my face and closed my eyes.

I must have slept for about an hour and woke to find the wind had lifted the towel off my legs; I was now very badly sunburnt. Nothing for it. My time on the beach was over. I sought what shade I could near the small café and spent some time rubbing various ointments and lotions on my glowing legs. All very painful. I soon found that sunburn takes the energy out of you.

We idled back up the track towards the town, wondering what to do next. We decided to make that beach our home for our stay on the island.

'Look out, lads. It's him!' John spotted a small dapper figure heading our way.

'Dodge him, Richard, dodge him.'

We slipped round a corner and managed to avoid Angelo. When he'd gone, we decided to explore the old windmill close to where we'd spent the night.

It was unlike any windmill we'd ever seen before. Like a pointed straw hat, a rough-thatched roof sat on top of a white-washed round structure. There seemed to be only one narrow doorway and a small window close under the thatch. Windmills at home had four or five broad wooden sails with vanes inset to catch the wind. This windmill was a cross between a spider's web and a bicycle wheel. It had about ten spokes linked round the perimeter by wires or strong ropes. In between these spokes were slung small triangular sheets, like ships' pennants or sails on a child's model boat. They hardly seemed sufficient to catch the wind.

'What do you think?' Chris said. 'Shall we?'

'Why not? It's free.'

We hunched through the doorway into the dark. Inside we found narrow stairs twisting up inside the tower. We started climbing.

'Mind your heads,' Mike said.

Just above us, near the top of the stairs, we encountered a massive wooden beam capable of giving a nasty bruise. The landing itself had rickety rough-hewn boards. Here the owner greeted us with a smile and, with elaborate gestures, motioned us to sit down on bags of flour stacked against the curved wall. We leaned back and watched a huge creaking wheel above us driving, by means of wooden teeth, an enormous grinding spindle which came down to the central trough. The hopper delivering the grain was gravity-fed and also made of wood. Again the owner gestured and showed us a slow trickle of grey flour coming out from under the millstone.

'Amazing,' Mike said, 'the whole thing dependent on the wind.' In that dark, creaking structure of wood and stone, we sampled a fascinating world of serenity, strength and timelessness.

We thanked the miller as best we could and set off down the steep stairs. Already I could feel the ache of sunburn on my stiffening legs.

We emerged blinking into the late afternoon light. Above us the mill sails continued turning at the pace of centuries.

'What an extraordinary place.' Chris was again busy with his camera.

'And for once the bloody Greeks haven't seen it as a chance to fleece the tourists.'

Later, we sat round a small table at the *Apollon* restaurant down on the waterfront, waiting for our evening meal; by now we were all ravenous.

'Must get windy here,' Chris said. 'See how all the tablecloths are tied onto the tables?'

'You wouldn't think so from the slow turning of the windmill, though, would you?' I replied. Then I remembered how my legs became sore.

'Look at that, lads.'

Games and Sordid Shouting Matches

At the table next to ours was the tame pelican of Mykonos, Peter. He wandered freely amongst the diners, obviously tolerated by the restaurants, but a damn nuisance if you wanted a quiet meal. He kept on trying to snatch food from our neighbours' table with his long beak. In the end to avoid his pestering, the diners threw him a fish head which landed on the ground nearby. Peter tried desperately to pick it up, craning his neck to extraordinary angles and putting his head on one side. But he was unsuccessful. His long beak just pushed the fish head under one of the chairs.

At this point a feral kitten appeared, also foraging. He managed to get much closer to the fish head but was equally unsuccessful, since Peter cut off his offensive by trapping his front paws in his beak. I was reminded of Aesop's fable of The Stork and the Fox where neither creature managed to eat a proper meal.

We lingered at our table, even sampled some Ouzo again. But someone there taught us a new Greek phrase, useful if we were going to do any bargaining: πολυ 'ακριβω (poly acrivo) – too expensive.

The light began turning grey; the sun sinking into banks of clouds. We wondered what to do next. John had already started yawning and thinking of kip.

'I say, do you fancy joining us in a game of hide and seek round the streets of

Mykonos?' Stephen Duckworth, baby-faced and looking like an eager owl, blinked at us through his spectacles.

A hesitation. We looked at each other quizzically.

'No, count me out,' John said. 'I'm knackered.'

'Me, too.' Mike stretched and yawned.

We declined to join the game and all four of us began to stagger back up the hill past the windmills and down to our beach. Time for an early night. I could feel my legs glowing under my trousers and the skin felt so tight I thought it might split.

★ ★ ★

Saturday 15th August

We woke late the next morning, each waiting for someone else to make a move. Chris wriggled first out of his sleeping bag and literally took the plunge – straight into the sea; Mike chased him and the two splashed and laughed together.

John, however, sat up, yawned, put his specs on and reached for his cigarettes. I was in no mood for dashing about. I searched through my rucksack and fetched out the most protective clothes I could find. No shorts for me! I eased my aching, sunburnt limbs into trousers and a long-sleeved shirt, covering up for the day.

The beach restaurant had basic toilets which we made use of and I soon discovered yesterday's lunchtime diet of chocolate and fresh fruit was remarkably effective as a laxative.

The owner of the beach restaurant was just opening up. Dark-haired, a face set with angry stubble and wearing the ubiquitous short-sleeved white shirt, he called me over.

'You boys hungry?'

As usual, living out in all that fresh air, we'd soon be starving. 'Yes, probably,' I said.

'I undercut town. I give you break-fast for eight drachmas.' He held up eight fingers.

'Eight drachmas each?'

'Of course.'

'I'll have to ask my friends.'

'Ok. I give you good break-fast.'

A short debate ensued. Mike and Chris were now out of the sea and towelling themselves down. As always we converted the cost back into English money.

'That's not bad,' said Chris. 'Let's do it. Only two bob each.'

When we were all ready, we sat down underneath the awning of the café. Already the sun was climbing.

Breakfast arrived – one and a half slices of hard bread with a meagre supply of butter and honey; the Nescafé tasted of aniseed.

'God, you can tell we're not in Athens!'

'I'm still ravenous,' I said.

'Me, too. That's not worth eight drachmas.' Chris was feeling belligerent.

'What's in this coffee? It tastes like that bloody ouzo stuff,' Mike said. 'I tell you what. I reckon it's about time we put a stop to accepting swindles and being cheated.'

'I agree.' Chris stood up. 'We haven't had fair value. What do you think? Six each?'

Mike and Chris began collecting twenty four drachmas.

'I don't know,' I said. I felt we'd committed ourselves to the eight drachmas and refrained from joining the battle.

John too was doubtful. 'I don't know, lads, we did agree eight.'

'Twenty four drachmas.' Mike thrust the money at the man. 'Food not good. Bread stale.'

'No, you must pay me eight drachmas each. I fetch police.' The bar owner glared at us.

'No, twenty four drachmas is all it's worth. Take it.' Mike plonked the notes and four drachma coins onto the table and he and Chris walked off.

'No, you pay nothing. You not like my food, you pay nothing.' The bar owner pushed the money into my hand as I sat on the low wall of the restaurant.

We were dangerously near a division in our own camp now. I felt it was worth thirty two drachmas to keep his goodwill for the use of the facilities. A tap and a toilet were always handy.

Eventually John yielded and by a majority decision we decided to leave twenty four drachmas and go.

'Where is he now?' Mike said.

'He stalked off up the slope towards the town,' John said. 'I watched him go.'

'Do you think he's gone to get the police?' Somewhat apprehensive, we all began packing our rucksacks, and I rolled up my lilo and fastened it under the top straps.

The man returned after five minutes and we knew we'd called his bluff; he hadn't time to reach the police or even phone them.

Now we marched in twos through the shelter and put the twenty four drachmas down on a table.

'Twenty four drachmas.' Chris spoke with an air of authority and finality. Then we turned and walked away in an impression of unity.

'No, no!' The man tried to throw the money into the metal cup dangling from John's sleeping bag. The coins chinked into it, bounced out and fell to the floor.

We kept on walking.

The last we saw of the barman was a small figure grovelling on the floor to pick up the money and save what notes he could from the wind.

The Greek Pace of Life

Back in the main town, around the harbour area, we began exploring the streets which twisted up the hillside in gentle slopes and steps, away from Mykonos harbour. They were little more than alleyways, more suited to donkeys with pannier baskets than to any motor vehicle. Everywhere, white-washed walls hemmed in the streets, and any mortar between the stones or cobbles also glistened with white paint. We soon discovered how possible the previous night's game of hide-and-seek would have been. We often struggled to find our way; our arrival on the first night showed that. We began to think it impossible to take the same route twice. Someone remarked that the best way of finding a particular back-street shop was not to look for it.

The only buildings with colour were the many chapels set at intervals around the town. Their roofs was usually a reddish pink, brighter than terracotta, though we did see an occasional blue dome. Woodwork on the houses was left unpainted. Doors, window frames and banisters remained in natural wood. Occasionally they were varnished.

In photographs, and from a distance, the square buildings and glistening walls made Mykonos appear a modern city; a closer look at the worn marble steps and the tumbledown doorways showed that the black-clothed peasants and the little donkeys tethered in odd corners lived in a poor town.

Its old-world charm attracted the more sophisticated visitors, probably because it was a stepping-off point for anyone wanting to visit the classical site on the island of Delos. But I reckoned the people I saw on the quay-front were secretly glad they didn't have to live their whole life in such surroundings;

they found the place delightful and quaint for a fortnight at the most. Much of the atmosphere on Mykonos reminded me then of Cornish insularity – the peasants stared and gossiped in the same suspicious, semi-friendly way.

We set off for a morning walk along a cliff road, again very similar to Cornwall, towards the famed San Stefano beach. The road hugged the line of the coast and the cliffs seemed merely troublesome hills. We were away from people and civilisation now and often stopped to take photos. The landscape, though picturesque, seemed dry and bare, with very few houses. We never reached the beach. Our meagre breakfast and our leisurely pace meant our bellies dictated we should turn back to civilisation. We returned

to the town, bought our own picnic and walked inland away from the harbour, settling for lunch under a tree near a fountain.

I remained there that afternoon away from the crowds, and in the shade. The others went back to the harbour to do more exploring. I sat on a low wall under the tree writing and catching up on my notes. Nearby was a dirty white wall where two basic brass taps protruded. A crude drainage channel set in the concrete ran beneath. The place was obviously much used since green-black mould spread up from the bottom of the wall almost to the taps themselves. Many people came to draw water. They brought old petrol cans, jugs, earthenware pitchers – even plastic boxes. They sat near me on the bench seats and chatted to each other; the tap had no cause to hurry. Many were old women, wrinkled and cadaverous, their brown faces and white hair contrasting strongly with their dark clothing – their arms still strong through long years of drudgery. Several people used the taps to wash their hair, and some came up in swimming costumes and sluiced the water liberally over themselves – another way of bathing.

One small boy came just to play. Barefoot, with black hair clipped short, he wore an immaculate white tee-shirt and dark blue rompers with cross-over straps and a bib front. He began playing with the taps, letting the water trickle into the gulley below. I

wanted a photo of him, so shouted 'Hoy!' to attract his attention. Startled, he looked back at me and guiltily turned the tap off. I had my picture.

Some of the island boys crowded round me as I sat there, looking over at my notebook. They seemed amazed I could write in characters other than Greek – perhaps that I could write at all.

Somehow we always managed to make contact across the language barrier, even if only by signs and miming. Antics, laughter, or a smile worked wonders. But Mike, who couldn't read the Greek characters on notices and shop signs, was becoming tired of the language. To him, when it was spoken quickly, it became nothing more than harsh chatter.

We rejoined forces at the harbour; Chris and John had stayed together, and both John and Mike had done sketches of various quaint parts. John, too, became the focus for curious small boys who wanted to see what he found interesting enough to draw.

Once together again, we also took on the Greek pace of life and just sat on the low harbour wall, chatting and idly watching the passers-by.

'Look there's that stupid bloke again!'

Ever since we'd first arrived in Mykonos, we'd taken a thorough dislike to a tall, self-important Greek. We'd first seen him pushing his way out of the ship's First Class Lounge in an attempt to queue-jump his way into the little boats to the shore. He carried then a multitude of underwater fishing equipment – goggles, flippers and a spear gun – all dangling casually from his arm. Something about his tall, nose-in-air arrogance and flaunted wealth made us all loathe him instantly.

All small places are claustrophobic and Mykonos was no exception. Escape from the island or other people was not easy. It'd been our misfortune to see this bronzed coxcomb often, strutting by on the quay-front in various stages of undress, showing off his oiled torso and legs. Frequently he had a fawning satellite, also slickly rigged out; sometimes he accompanied a woman he'd found.

'Take a photograph of him, Chris, as a reminder!' John said. 'We'll all show our reactions in the background.'

'Yes, we can have "hate" sessions back in college every time we look at his picture,' I added with enthusiasm.

Chris worked out a careful plan to capture us pulling faces and registering our disgust as the man ponced past.

'Quick get ready! He's coming!'

The scene was all set, our principal on stage. We were tense, ready for action.

'Ah, Reechard! I see you again. How are you?'

Angelo had sneaked up on our blind side.

Couldn't ignore him. He began ranging round our group, shaking hands, completely unaware of our tension, our poses. I had the double embarrassment of trying to play my part for Chris's picture and talk to Angelo. Hopeless! He was now centre stage and our opportunity for capturing a picture of our oily *bête noire* vanished. Chris lowered his camera and grimaced. We didn't think for one minute of photographing Angelo – now, when we look back, the most memorable character on our island trip.

'Ah, tonight, I ask myself why don't I eat with you boys? This very fine restaurant: good fried fish here.' Angelo indicated one of the quay-front restaurants where the waiters were starting to lay the tables.

We all stood around helpless; we had no *savoir faire* for such persistence. Saying a blank no would seem rude. I was aware of Chris and John turning away, trying to melt into the background. I knew already what they felt.

'Look, you two go off. That's all right.'

'Right-ho, then,' said Chris. 'What about you, Mike?'

'Think it best I stay with Richard, don't you?' His voice a discreet rumble.

We watched the other two set off. John would be getting hungry already.

'Reechard, say to me again what is your friend's name?'

I told him.

'Michael, Ma-ik. I will go get changed for dinner. You boys wait here at table. I come back soon.' He leaned forward and motioned he wanted to speak in my ear: 'You know, Reechard, it's not necessary for you to sleep on beaches like a beggar. I have another bed in my apartment. You could sleep there. More comfortable.'

'No, I'm fine, Angelo, honestly, we like sleeping outside.'

Mike and I watched him leave and began our wait at the table. Now the smell of frying fish caught at our sea-bred appetites.

'Thought we were going to sit straight down for a meal,' I said.

'Bloody Greeks, never know what to expect. What's that say?' He pointed at the menu.

'That's calamari.'

'No thanks. They can keep their bloody squid. Have they got swordfish?'

'Sure to have.'

We each had a small bottle of beer while we waited. I kept looking along the road to see if I could see Angelo.

'Bloody man, it's worse than waiting for a woman,' Mike said. 'We can't sit here all night.'

'Ten more minutes, mate, then we'll eat.'

'Bugger's been half an hour already.'

When Angelo appeared, he was dressed completely in blue: short-sleeved shirt, neatly pressed trousers and blue deck shoes. He came in, wafting a cloud of submissive fragrance.

'Ah, boys! I find you again.' He prepared to sit down, then turned suddenly, waved, and fluted 'Hello!' to two other young men nearby. 'Ah, tonight I am lucky. Those two English boys are jealous because this time I sit here with you.'

'You know them, do you?' I said by way of conversation. 'I'm sorry we've already eaten. We weren't sure whether you were coming or not. We were very hungry.'

'I understand. My bath takes much time for hot water. I'm sorry for your wait.'

He raised his hand, caught a waiter's attention, said something rapidly in Greek and a bottle of white wine and some glasses appeared on the table.

If we didn't know before, we began now to have a pretty good idea what we were dealing with. On the boat, I had suspicions he was queer – a term we used then; now I was convinced because of the scent that surrounded him after his bath. Deodorants and aftershaves had scarcely reached England.

Angelo poured all of us some wine and we clinked glasses.

'You know, Reechard, youth is the best thing in life.' He squeezed my arm affectionately and stared straight into my eyes. 'Look at you, you are lucky. You have youth, you are young in spite of this.' He tugged at the wispy growth of beard on my cheek and laughed. 'Sometimes I feel one hundred years old.' He turned and gave a flick of his fingers at Mike's dark, flop-down quiff. 'And Ma-ik, Ma-ik, you too have youth.'

Angelo's light meal arrived and he began picking at it, breaking off frequently to tug my beard and laugh, or flick Mike's hair. Always he rolled his eyes lasciviously like some ancient satyr at play. Mike said later that he had to endure Angelo playing kneesy with him underneath our small table. His stares were difficult to avoid.

We had to do something. 'Angelo,' I said, 'will you do something for me?'

'Of course, Reechard, what I can.'

'When you have finished, I wonder... Will you help me buy a skirt for my girlfriend?'

Silence. His eyes stood still at last, and his face fell.

'Reechard has a *girl* friend?' He looked at me hard and could see the truth in my face. Then he changed.

His attitude seemed like a rapid jump to the guns.

'Reechard has a girl friend!' He clinked his glass against mine with almost savage gusto.

'What is she like this girl friend? Is she beautiful? How old is she?' He was struggling to believe me. I mumbled some answers and then stood up.

We'd already paid for our meal, and I decided the only thing to do was to take the initiative and make Angelo follow. We'd go souvenir buying.

'Wait till you get to Mykonos, and buy your gifts there,' someone had said. 'Don't pay Athens' prices.' Everywhere we went we saw the latest gimmick – a bright, multi-coloured woollen bag in various Greek patterns. Horizontal stripes, sea monsters, even ancient monuments. I couldn't tell whether they were knitted or crocheted and didn't much like them, but each had a long, almost rope-like handle to hang from the shoulder and knitted ends which tufted out at the bottom. They were everywhere, and I soon determined I wouldn't buy one of these garish mini sacks.

At some point, however, I decided I wanted to buy Greek skirt material for my girl friend at home. We dived into the nearest folk-weave seller, I cast around hastily and lighted on a skirt length that would do. Green, I thought, will go with her red hair. It must have been one-size-fits-all and wasn't quite what I wanted, but I decided it was better to ride the crest of the wave and use Angelo as a bargaining agent.

A rapid exchange of Greek followed where he haggled for me and then a price was agreed.

'You know, Reechard, for you on your own that would have cost two hundred drachmas. Now you have it for one hundred ten drachmas.' He smiled in triumph.

'Yes, thank you very much.'

At sixty-five drachmas I saw a scarf as a present for someone else and asked Angelo's help again. He got me another discount and I bought the two items together for one hundred and seventy drachmas. I was pleased with my bargains. The two items would certainly have cost much more than £2 at home.

I learned from Angelo that night. He was extremely charming and laughed and joked with the seller while they haggled. It was a game to them both. Our English attitude would have been to try to beat the price down as if expecting to be cheated. From him I learned that if possible one should 'knock down' the Greeks in a jovial, not a belligerent, way.

I thanked him very much for his help. Mike continued to look around, uncertain what to buy. While we stood waiting, I told Angelo about our *contretemps* over the morning's breakfast.

'No, that was right, Reechard. It is good that you pay only twenty four drachmas. Some Greeks are greedy.'

Darkness was settling over the island now. Each little shop had a small cavern of goods and souvenirs inside under crude electric light; outside more garments hung on rails or the back of the doors, illuminated by high pressure paraffin lamps which flared light into the gathering darkness.

Mike decided he wanted to buy himself a shirt and we walked practically next door to look at the selection. I could see a problem developing, however: both he and Angelo were drawn to the same red-brown and gold shirt. Angelo continued his laughter and banter with anyone who caught his eye, including the shopkeeper. In the end, Mike cut across all that, bought the shirt and beat Angelo to it. It wasn't clear from all his joviality that Angelo had been bargaining and seriously intended to buy the shirt for himself.

When Mike understood what had happened he became very English and muttered his apology. 'I'm sorry, Angelo, I didn't realise…'

'No, no! Do not worry, my friend. I am sure it will look much better on a young person. You must have it.'

I was impressed then by his generosity and charm, the gracious way he deferred to Mike. Even so I felt it important we should keep him on the move. It felt better being in control. In the same boutique I bought a second scarf, and again Angelo got me discount – a reduction of five drachmas from forty five to forty.

After our purchases, time for a coffee. I was amazed to see Angelo put three spoonfuls of Nescafé in his cup before pouring on boiling water. Mike and I, by contrast, had small cups of sludgy black liquid – what we still called *Turkish* coffee.

Angelo's conversation returned frequently to my *girl* friend in vague tones of disbelief.

'No, it's right,' said Mike, 'her name is Meg which in English is short for Margaret.'

We became increasingly mischievous and started making jokes at his expense. When he asked Mike what he planned to do as a career, Mike replied that he was training to be a doctor.

'So one day you will be able to doctor me, perhaps.'

'I could Angelo, most certainly,' he replied in a voice heavy with significance. He grinned at me.

We started making references to *little boy blue,* looking at this eager diminutive figure, holding court at our table and dressed in his evening best.

'Yes, come blow up your horn,' I said.

Mike honked his laugh.

'Ah, boys, it is good for me to have laughter, the friendship of youth.'

He was good company when he stopped flirting and talked sensibly about ballet, for example, though he did weary us with his frequent stories about himself as Maître Grymanis.

We wondered how we'd manage to part from him that evening, particularly after his invitation to me earlier. But he accepted our leave-taking without much difficulty.

'When shall I see you again, my friends?'

'I'm not sure, Angelo,' I replied. 'We don't know what the others are doing.'

'All right, I see you again soon. Now I wish you goodbye. It will not be pleasant sleeping outside tonight. I have nice comfortable bed, Reechard.'

I laughed and we set off up the hill over the headland towards our Ayios Iannis beach on the other side. As the darkness swallowed us up, Mike looked back.

'Don't think he's following us,' he said.

We arrived back at the beach at about 11.15 PM to find two snuggling heaps on the dark sand. A surprise to find that the others had already turned in for the night since our evening seemed to go very quickly.

An unpleasantly strong wind had sprung up – apparently a common thing in the Cyclades. Angelo must have known or read the signs. Mike and I began to unpack our sleeping bags and prepare for bed. The two heaps stirred and moved with us into the shelter of a wall. Even so Angelo was proved right: it was an uncomfortable night with high wind, and sand settling in every possible chink of our sleeping bags.

Dry Wind and Brown Grass

Sunday 16th August

'Look at all this,' grumbled John, 'it's even in my specs case.'
We all shook out our sleeping bags, trying to dispel the gritty sand. Still fairly early, but it was our D-day – when we planned to land on Delos. We didn't know what to expect. We knew it was an island and one of Greece's most famous archaeological sites.

'Which god is supposed to have been born there?' Mike began rolling up his sleeping bag.

'Apollo,' I replied, squeezing the last traces of air out of my lilo. They merged into the wind with a discreet sigh.

'Still blowing. Hope the sea's not too rough.' Chris leaned on one elbow against the wall which had been our windbreak for the night. 'It's something like a mile away, over there somewhere.' He pointed towards the west.

'Now what are we going to do about brekkers, lads?' John breathed loudly on his spectacles and polished them with the tail of his navy shirt. He screwed his dark beret on. 'Right! Ready.'

We began trudging up the hill away from the beach, lugging our rucksacks.

I'd given up trying to comb my sea-stiffened hair. I let the wind sweep it back from my forehead like a dark wave breaking over my head. I paused, scratched my growth of beard, and plodded behind the others. I wore my white shirt with the sleeves rolled down and my khaki drills: my sunburnt legs still hurt.

We knew we'd have to stock up on food for our stay there. Delos was uninhabited – only one tourist pavilion to cater for our needs, open only during tourist hours. We'd be camping on the island until midday the next day.

Somewhere in Mykonos town a church bell tolled. We managed some stale currant rolls from the bakery, bought a large hunk of dry, grey bread – and some grapes. That would have to do.

'Is that it? Is that our transport?' We saw a couple of fishing boats rolling and jostling at anchor in the harbour. Chris later described ours as *a cranky motor boat which also used sail*. We wobbled our way across a gang plank and found somewhere

to sit on the benches around the outside of the boat. It already seemed crowded and uncomfortable. There was a rectangular compartment which housed the engine and, jutting up from it, a dirty white funnel with a couple of blue stripes on it. The Greek colours, perhaps. I was fascinated by the slow, hollow thud of the engine, the sound emerging from that funnel – a lazy dud, dud, dud. It scarcely seemed to have the power to take us across the water. At the stern, an ancient fisherman scanned the sea ahead: flat peaked cap, grey drooping moustache and cigarette. One hand for the tiller, the other for a rope he never released. I had no idea what it was for. He looked like a one-time member of the resistance: lean, leathered skin and scruffy clothes.

Dud, dud, dud.

We cleared the shelter of Mykonos harbour and our boat began pitching to the swell and lash of the waves. The wind skimmed the cream off the breakers and stung our faces. Everywhere I looked, the passengers held on to something to steady themselves: the engine housing, the side of the boat, the rigging. One older man in jacket and formal trousers held his trilby hat crammed on his head.

The smell of diesel oil and fish swirled around us.

The gaffer in the stern was very much a character. Head up, he adjusted his cap and stared clear-eyed into the mid distance like an Old Testament prophet. I was fascinated to see how the motor's pulse ran through him, watched him judder up and down to the piston's slow throb as if even he was part of the boat.

At one point he and the other two crew hauled up the sail and the boat bounced and splashed its way forward. After forty minutes, we arrived at the landing stage on Delos. A small, newly-built stone pier jutted out into deep, clear water. At last the sea and our stomachs settled. One of the crew leaped off the bow of the boat, a wooden box under his arm, and began heaving and hauling on a rope while the boat's engine puttered to retain position. The young man strained to get a foothold against a metal bollard and held the bow steady. One by one we stepped over the side of the boat, onto the box, and land at last.

'I'm glad that's over,' John said. 'Did you feel sick?'

Mike harrumphed. 'No, I was OK, actually.'

Almost immediately, we started to climb.

New-built stone steps ascended in a broad path up from the rock. Optimistic, we began the long upward walk to the tourist pavilion. We could leave our baggage there in safety while we explored.

Everywhere the terrain was dry and bare. An unrelenting brown teased the eye in that rocky, barren place. Everywhere bleached of colour. Occasionally coarse grass and spiky plants with yellow flowers tugged and shook in the strong, unremitting wind.

Birthplace of Apollo? I thought. This is the most God-forsaken place I've ever been to.

We eased off our rucksacks, stacked them in a corner of the tourist pavilion and, equipped only with cameras and sketch  pads, set out for a trek to the highest point. The island seemed totally flat except where it swelled to a small peak, 113m high: Mount Kythnos.

From the summit, the island looked like a half-finished model. No structures stood tall; a few weak columns stubbed up from the surrounding brown; cleared areas with the outline of buildings reminded me of bomb sites. This archaeological treasure was proclaimed as important as Delphi or Athens, a must-do on any tour of Greece. French archaeologists had worked here since the 1870s, excavating and revealing the many Greek and Roman remains which jumbled and jostled for space on the island. I turned away disenchanted; the Minoan remains at Cnossos had spoiled me. I could believe in the reality that people actually lived there once. Delos, however, was left *au naturel,* and I came up against my limits as a Classical scholar: I hated the place when I should have revelled in it.

Below and all round us, the sea glittered mercilessly. No shelter, no shade. Chris took out his camera and captured panoramic shots of the landscape; the others fooled around. They leaned into the wind and peered out to sea like latter-day explorers searching for a sail, some sign of life.

'Amazing to find remains even up here,' Mike said. He trod with caution over a frayed mosaic pavement which edged towards a steep drop at the top of the hill.

Delos demanded effort, and I wasn't prepared to give it. If we'd had a book or a map, I might have lent it some concentration and made sense of it all. As it was, we were just looking at a muddle of old stones. The others went off exploring, I spent the rest of my day writing in the shade of the veranda of the tourist pavilion, glad to escape into my own world and away from all this hot melancholy.

As the sun turned down its heat in late afternoon, I took a brief look round the island's museum. I quickly considered it poor, its layout jumbled. I preferred statues, anyway, to fragments of columns or tombs. But nothing was certain, nothing defined. A Roman figure glared at me.

Who's that? I wondered.

Mithridates? the card replied. They didn't know either.

Even more inane was another label which just said: *Statue d'homme.*

Obvious, I thought, looking at the anatomy.

The other three were away a long time, still wandering.

I looked at the souvenirs in the tourist shop. Much more expensive than on Mykonos, but there were much prettier skirts.

Damn.

I decided to have a quick look round the site itself. I wandered away, seeking to investigate anything that was taller than me. My cultural grump remained. First impressions were that I was viewing a pile of junk and rubbish. I wracked my brains to remember what I knew about Delos. The Lions. Even at school I'd seen pictures of the famous Lions of Delos. I'd

go and look for them. Eventually I found a broad avenue with several squatting, snarling marble lions. I knew they were old, but they didn't look like any lions I recognised. Not Trafalgar Square stuff. These were long, slender, stylised. They could have been dinosaurs or seals, their stone faces worn rough by the weather of two thousand five hundred years. Now they gaped rather than roared at the world.

Mm, famous, but not fabulous, I decided, and began heading back.

'Are you hungry, Pike? I'm starving.' John strode into where I was sitting, his teeth set in a broad grin. We'd made a poor picnic during the day with the stuff we'd brought from Mykonos. We felt hungry; we were thirsty. Now was time for a good meal in the one restaurant on the island. As usual we were served out of doors.

'God, this bloody wind,' said Chris. 'It's coming straight off the sea.'

I looked at John's arms in his short-sleeved shirt. Goose pimples showed, and the hairs riffled in the strong breeze.

'I shan't be long for my pit,' he said.

'Me neither,' said Mike. 'I'm knackered.'

'Hate this hot dry air.'

We climbed up the stairs to the roof of the tourist pavilion and bedded down fairly rapidly.

Fifteen hours to go, I thought, and settled deeper into my sleeping bag.

You Die This Night?

Monday 17th August

The sun glanced red across the sea and began to climb. We all stirred awake on the roof of the tourist pavilion. Still early: a chill in the air. Purple haze along the horizon.

'No good, lads. I need the bog.' John crammed his glasses on, struggled out of his sleeping bag and stumbled down the stairs to the only toilet on Delos.

'Hurry up, John,' I called. 'I need to follow you.'

'Me, too,' said Mike. 'Feels like the galloping gut rot.'

Three of us with violent stomach upsets. What had we eaten? Or drunk? Little natural water existed on the island.

Chris, however, had no symptoms and seemed happy.

John reappeared and slumped against the parapet of the roof terrace.

'Don't be long. I'm going to have to go again,' he said.

Downstairs, in that dingy concrete cubicle, I vomited and had diarrhoea, then returned exhausted to the roof.

Mike took his turn. 'I'm wondering if it's dysentery,' he said, when he returned. 'Must make sure we don't get dehydrated.'

I reached for my water bottle and took a swig. But I couldn't even keep water down. Now, feeling thoroughly weak and miserable, I made several journeys down those steps.

For some time all three of us took it in turns to besiege the toilet. Chris stood by patiently, even ate a little stale-bread breakfast.

Mike, who in different circumstances might have launched into his Goon Show imitation of Major Bloodnok suffering from the Bombay belly, sat subdued, gazing across to the sea.

One by one the others began to move off down to ground level, exploring, sketching, photographing. I stayed hunched on the roof unwilling to move far. In case.

John reappeared: 'How are you feeling, Pike? I've found walking round helps. Try it.'

'Yeah, I might in a minute. But don't wait for me. You lot go off if you want to. I'll be OK.'

When my insides felt more stable, I too set off and staggered literally round the site, often sitting down in what shade I could find.

In spite of my weakness, my impressions were more favourable this time. Always accompanied by a nagging ache in the gut, I made a brief trip round most of the Roman remains which were not too far from the pavilion and its toilet. Around me, bright green lizards scampered and darted into crevices in the stones. I could definitely sense wide streets now, paved with what looked like giant cobbles, but the houses seemed strangely formal, not easy to relax in: fragments of mosaic floors, narrow rooms with thick walls. No trace of furniture or comfort to make it come alive for me.

Down one of the avenues, I came across another of the famous sights of Delos: white marble pedestals, sentinels along the route, with the remains of huge, erect stone phalluses perched on top. Each one had been chopped off a little above its root as if some prudish censor had taken exception to these rampant fertility symbols.

I didn't feel up to much myself and began to make my way back towards the pavilion. I still felt weak and the sun was getting hotter. But I did notice with some interest that the archaeologists used a horse-drawn excavation train when they worked on part of the site. They needed to move debris away in order to reveal new treasures, and some poor nags hauled these wagons along rickety rails. No sign of the beasts, of course. Too hot for digging in the middle of summer.

Fancy bringing horses or donkeys over from Mykonos in those tiny boats, I thought.

No sign of the others when I returned to the pavilion. Exhausted now, I crept up onto the roof and slept soundly in what little shade the parapet afforded.

Eventually the chatter and tramp of a new day's tourists woke me, and I realised the boat to take us back had arrived. I dreaded the thought of that rolling return to Mykonos. Now the time to leave had arrived, I seemed to be the only weak member of our party. Sounds drifted up from downstairs; the pavilion shop was opening up for the latest batch of souvenir hunters.

Time to go.

The pitching and plunging of the boat journey back was even more violent. It didn't help that many of the passengers moved over to one side of the boat to get shelter from the spray that the strong wind flung across us. Their movement unbalanced the boat and emphasised the rolling movement.

'I feel sick.' John looked pale and subdued.

I clung on grimly, scarcely aware of our journey.

With relief, we arrived back in Mykonos harbour. I was surprised to find my stomach seemed much better for the trip; I felt fitter than some of the others. Nevertheless, I wasn't well and kept on shivering. I wanted somewhere to rest, some refuge from the scouring heat, didn't want to go back to our beach or trek around the town for several hours. Where could I go?

Eventually Mike and I both decided we'd head for the Tourist Police Station which was close to the quay and, appropriately, also near the public toilets.

We were all aware of this special police force, different from the law-enforcing ’αστυνομια (astynomia), but so far hadn't had much call for them. They were supposed to be helpful but we'd found them pretty useless. As far as I was concerned they were masters of the Gallic shrug. But where else could we turn?

'You can go here,' said the officer, carefully masked by his dark glasses. He gestured towards the concrete floor. Mike and I looked at each other and realised it was our best option. A busy place: constant visitors asking questions or wanting directions, backpackers dropping off their kit or coming back to collect it. But the place was out of the sun, marginally cooler than the midday furnace outside.

Carefully we unrolled our sleeping bags and stretched out. It felt as though we lay in the middle of the cramped room. But we didn't care, managed to shut the world out, and both of us slept soundly. John and Chris, since it was now time, went off to find some lunch and left us to it. At some point I discovered I had a temperature of 100 degrees and knew then that I was far from well. Dysentery? Sunstroke? It didn't matter. I just needed to be well enough to catch the boat out that evening.

The others returned from shopping, looked in and went away again when it was obvious we were still not ready to join them.

'I don't think I can eat, mate,' I said to Mike, 'but I feel I need something to keep my strength up.'

Mike cleared his throat in his best doctor mode. 'Glucose probably won't hurt, and maybe some aspirin to get your temperature down.'

We agreed we'd go outside and try and find a chemist we'd spotted previously. Needless to say we struggled to locate the shop and wandered the hot streets in the westering sun for some time. Then back to our floor. This time Mike left me to it and went off. I crunched up two aspirins without water, lay down and slept again.

I woke, bathed in sweat, dimly aware that a group of people were standing over me looking down.

Heavy shoes, bare legs, leather shorts.

Germans.

One tall, blond-haired youth looked down at me and smirked: 'You die this night, huh?'

I bleared back at him and said nothing.

Feet scuffing on the concrete, they tramped out of the building.

My next visitor was Angelo.

'Ah, poor Reechard, you are not well. What is matter with you?'

I heaved myself up onto my elbow, agreeing I wasn't feeling too good and described some of my symptoms. 'How did you know I was here?'

'I saw your friends – not Maik – the other boys, and the tall one with the spectacles he told me where I shall find you.'

Thanks, John.

I seemed to be surrounded by hundreds of doctors all contradicting each other as to what treatment I should have.

Cold water bandage on the head… Drink plenty water… Take more aspirin… Eat nothing for two days.

I smiled feebly. It was enough to make me get up and leave the place.

'Ah, Reechard is a little delicate, I think.'

Delicate Reechard became a catchphrase among us for some time afterwards.

It seemed Angelo was fated to follow us. He explained he too was heading for the Island of Syros, our next destination on the way back to Athens. He'd obviously be on the same boat.

'I will return, Reechard, when I have booked my ticket for the ship.'

He did not, however, return, and I decided he'd begun to realise we weren't such chums after all.

Early evening now, and John and Chris went off for a meal before we went on board ship.

'I could do with a wash, mate,' Mike said. Together we packed up our things and finally left the tourist police station.

We headed for the public toilets near the water's edge, knowing there were rudimentary basins there.

Although we needed no toilet paper, our plans were unacceptable to the one-armed attendant. He wanted money; we had no small change. Another shouting match.

'Sod this,' Mike said. 'There's a fountain over there.' Very few people walked past so we stripped to the waist and washed our faces and necks thoroughly and patted ourselves dry with our swimming towels. I felt fresher, but not much better.

'They're over there,' I said spotting John and Chris eating. We went and joined them, though Mike and I had only water.

So far, so good, I thought, as I managed to keep the chilled water down.

Angelo also sat at a nearby table, accompanied by a slender girl.

'Makes a change.' Mike squeezed the words out of the side of his mouth.

'Hallo, boys. This Elena, one of my pupils. She also make holiday here and we did not know.'

He seemed much cooler towards John and Chris and scarcely acknowledged them.

'And so, Reechard, Maik, tonight you make journey to Athens again. I see you there, perhaps. Let me give you my address. You come visit me.'

'Well, thank you very much, Angelo. Very kind, but we don't know what our plans are.'

'We're probably going round the Peloponnese,' Mike said, in support.

'I think we'd better say goodbye now, Angelo.' I held out my hand and he shook it. I nodded to his companion.

'Goodbye, Reechard, I hope you feel better health soon. Good voyage to Athens and happy holidays.' He smiled at Mike weakly and shook his hand.

I thought he seemed saddened.

Our plans were to get off and stay one night on the island of Syros on our way back to Athens. Chris had discovered where to buy the tickets for our return journey and went to the only agent for our shipping company on the island.

'Yes, boat leave nine o'clock.'

Down on the long quayside a queue jostled and surged. We joined it at 8.15 PM.

'Is this the queue for *Despina*?' Chris was anxious to check because two boats were due to sail that evening.

'*Despina,* 'εν ταξει (it sounded like endaxi)

'It's OK.' He turned to us, relieved.

'And how are you two lovely lads now?' John beamed bonhomie.

'Still feeling feak and weeble,' I replied.

'Bloody Greeks. Don't understand the purpose of queues at all.' Mike flared as we watched other passengers push past us. Our tempers got shorter as rucksacks seemed to get heavier. We'd had enough.

The lights of the ship anchored in deep water looked calm and welcoming in the

gathering darkness. Another surge as the crowd heaved towards a place where the fishing boat tenders would take us to the ship. Eventually we were bobbing our way towards the waiting vessel.

As we scrambled aboard, I noticed the name on one of the ship's lifebelts: *Canares*. The ship slipped away into the darkness and stopped eventually, as expected, at Tinos. Then the trouble started.

'He's going to want to see our tickets,' John said.

A man came round checking everybody's documents. When he reached us, he paused, frowned and then spoke in voluble French.

'What's the matter?' Mike said.

'I think we're on the wrong boat, after all, chaps. This one doesn't stop at Syros. We're going straight back to Piraeus.' Chris kept his annoyance in check.

'Oh, bloody hell.'

More negotiations in French.

The man insisted we pay the full fare from Mykonos to Piraeus. Our tickets weren't valid on the *Canares* because it was owned by a different shipping company. He wouldn't even let us make up the difference from Syros.

He reached for an invoice book complete with carbon paper for on-the-spot tickets and laboriously rolled the sheets over to a fresh page; he took out a biro and scribbled new travel documents for the four of us. We all had to reach for our wallets and pay again.

'What's it say?' asked Mike.

'Dunno, it's bloody Greek handwriting.'

'We must reclaim our other fare when we get to Piraeus.' John sounded indignant.

'Merci!' The man walked off, making his way further along the deck.

'Sodding Greeks,' Mike raged, 'always so bloody casual.'

'And inefficient,' I added. 'They told us we were in the right queue.'

'Well, we don't get to see another Greek island, chaps. I'm sorry about that. We'll be back in Athens a day early.' Chris sounded matter of fact but was obviously disappointed.

I wasn't too upset by this forced change of plan. Apart from managing to avoid Angelo, I still felt queasy and not up to doing much. In fact five or six days passed before I felt reasonably fit again. Also all of us were tired and pretty dirty…

I described my adventures in a letter home to my girl-friend, Meg:

'The only thing I seem to need protection from is Greek queers! That really was an extraordinary experience…The trouble is everybody's now saying I attract them like flies! They're a bit afraid of letting me out of their sight at the moment in case I work up some more difficult situations. The trouble is that the Greeks, if they take a liking to you, are incredibly friendly and generous. It takes some time, I think, to decide if their intentions are anything other than usual.'

He's Done It Again!

Tuesday 18th August
Our boat docked at Piraeus at 5.30 AM – still too early to do anything or go anywhere. We were lucky to find a café open in the harbour area and decided on an early breakfast. We managed to spin it out for an hour and a half until the shipping offices opened. I still felt unwell and tagged along without complaint. Chris and John were particularly keen to try and get money refunded for the journey we'd missed from Mykonos to Syros.

From our table we had a good view of the arrivals at the port.

'Well, blow me,' Chris said, 'isn't that Valerie and whatsit?'

'Ann,' I said.

'Yes. What are they doing here?'

Valerie Kesterton and Ann Brazier were the two girls who'd be joining us in the hire-car to go round the Peloponnese. Cramming six of us in would spread the costs. We'd last seen them on Mykonos.

'How have you got here?' John said.

'We've just come off the *Despina*,' Valerie said.

'You haven't! That's the boat we should have been on.'

'Yes, we picked it up at Syros, about midnight.'

'Well, let's work it out,' Chris said. 'That means it must have left Mykonos at about 10.30.'

'Right, that does it.' John seemed cross now. 'The agent told us the *Despina* was due at 9.00 PM. That's why we joined the queue and got on the boat.'

'Bloody Greeks,' muttered Mike.

'I think we've got a pretty good case for getting our money back. Good job we met you,' Chris said.

'Well, best of luck,' Valerie said. 'See you later in the week.' The two girls walked off towards the metro back to Athens.

In the shipping office, the officials were not having any truck with our complaints.

'No, no, says on ticket – look, I show you, on back it say we no responsible if boat arrive late.'

'We accept that,' said Chris, 'but your agent told us the boat would be nine o'clock.'

'No. Is not possible. The boat schedule for 10.30. Look, I show you.' The man fetched out a grubby, tattered timetable and stabbed the time at Mykonos with his finger.

'Fair enough,' Mike rumbled in my ear.

'I just want to lie down,' I replied.

So we got no money back, but John and Chris did their best to maintain British dignity and stormed out in a huff.

★ ★ ★

Back at our hotel, we took advantage of a chance to wash all over and rid ourselves of the salt and sand of the Greek Islands. This can only have meant a strip wash at the basin, since there was no bath down the corridor for us to use. We must also have attempted rudimentary washing of socks, underpants and a shirt or two. They'd dry easily enough on the balcony of the room.

All of us slept again that morning, but I took the chance to collapse on my bed in that hot and noisy room and slept heavily for much of the day. My upset stomach no longer restricted me, but I felt poorly for the best part of a week. Because we'd arrived back in Athens early, we had two days to pass before we could set off on our car trip. Our treat of the day, as always, was to go out for our evening meal. More often than not we were drawn to the *Ideal* Restaurant where we liked the prices and the menu.

★ ★ ★

Wednesday 19th August

I still felt queasy the next day, but I made an effort to go out on my own into the city. I was particularly pleased to have a letter from 'home', from my girl-friend, Meg, who'd written to Cook's *Poste Restante* in Omonia Square. I produced my passport, and the clerk handed over the familiar Basildon Bond envelope.

Knowing also that it was my brother Steve's birthday in a few days, I spent some time trying to find a Greek card to send him. At last I found something suitable – not that it said Happy Birthday, as far as I could tell: Χρονια Πολλα. The equivalent of Many Happy Returns, I guessed. The only approximate translation I could come up with was Many Long-lasting Things!

We'd also decided we wouldn't take all our belongings round the Peloponnese. The car would be crowded anyway, with six of us and our luggage, so I decided to look for some packaging to leave my surplus stuff in. In one of the minor streets of Athens – I. Pesmatzoglou Street – which cut across some of the major roads radiating out from Omonia Square, I discovered a hardware store and went in to ask for carrier bags. I was worried how I'd communicate this idea and, as usual, was prepared to undertake mime if necessary. It was a relief to find the owner spoke good English and I complimented him on it. He impressed me with his friendliness and we shook hands. I soon learned his name was George Douzinas. A long conversation ensued on a wide range of subjects, punctuated also by comments from his dark-haired sister who kept appearing from a cubby hole at the rear of the shop.

'Guess how old I am,' she said.

I was just street-wise enough not to hazard a speculation as to her exact age. Older than me, I thought.

'Go on, you guess. I not very old.'

Politely I demurred, remembering Angelo had also asked me to guess his age. But she did say her name was Ellen. Thinking about it now, I guess she was probably Helena, but Greek pronunciation would not have sounded the initial 'h'. I had met Helen of Athens!

'After you come back from your trip in Peloponnese,' George took the lead again, 'you drop in here any time you want, and I take you out for very good Greek dinner with Greek wine.'

Back at the hotel I narrated my adventure to the others.

'He's done it again!' John burst out in horror.

'No I haven't,' I protested, but I did remember thinking the whole time I was speaking to George, *Is he or isn't he queer*? I didn't know, but I decided I'd follow up this invitation since he seemed pleasantly affable. 'Who knows?' I said, 'his sister may come too.'

Mike gave a mischievous grin: 'That's no guarantee. Sounds like he's the sort of bloke who sleeps with his sister.'

I described the adventure so far in a letter home to Meg:

Still I reckon it's all clocking it up for the old experience, and the others don't seem to have quite the same sort of adventures. Perhaps it's because they're always trotting off to look at things. I unfortunately can't meet any Ancient Greeks, so I have to make do with the Modern ones. Mike's properly cheesed off with the wogs. This is because a lot of this holiday has been mixing with the peasant class and their mentality. I think I've struck lucky with George Douzinas in being one of the few intelligent Greeks we've spoken to. Angelo was educated, but he had certain drawbacks which rather counterbalanced the attraction of talking to him.

★ ★ ★

Thursday 20th August
The day began with a mix-up. We all thought we were setting off for our tour of the Peloponnese today. 'Leave on the 20th' was firmly fixed in our minds. After breakfast, Mike set off to collect the car from Cooks and pick up the two girls who'd be joining us and sharing expenses. He walked round to the YWCA first where Valerie and Ann were staying but found only Ann. We'd apparently said clearly that we'd be leaving on *Friday* 20th – the right date, the wrong day. Valerie, believing we wouldn't be leaving until the Friday, had gone north to visit friends in Thessaloniki and wouldn't return until the evening.

'But she is flying back,' Mike said, when he broke the news to us. 'So we should all be OK tomorrow.' He'd returned without the car.

We now had to decide what to do with the extra day. The first thing was to ensure we could still sleep at the *Lux* that extra night. My stomach still felt queasy, and I didn't want to be far away from civilisation: Mike and I opted to stay in Athens for the day.

'Tell you what,' Chris said to John, 'we've seen most of the places we want to see in Athens. How do you fancy taking a bus out to Sunium?' They'd decided to go to *Cape Sounion* – a good forty-three-mile bus ride away from Athens.

John readily agreed, and we all said we'd meet up for dinner in the evening.

Mike and I spent the day mooching somewhat dispiritedly around the ancient sites of Athens. We went to the *agora* which I'd already dismissed as a heap of old stones, called in briefly to the reconstructed Stoa of Attalus at the south end of the site and found that to be another museum. Eventually, we wound our way up to the Acropolis and wandered around there again. I don't think I took any photographs; Mike probably did some sketching. I wish now that we'd all gone to Cape Sounion, but several factors intervened: tiredness after the travelling and tramping round Mykonos and Delos, my stomach upset and, no doubt, careful counting of pennies.

Chris' and John's bus took the inland route out to the Cape – a significant landmark in Greece and known since ancient times. Sunium, as we knew it, is the most southerly part of the mainland of Greece. It is their Land's End. Almost on the cliff edge, it seems, is the temple of Poseidon, still with eleven pillars standing. Byron came here – of course – and left his mark, deeply carved into the stone. And myth has it that this is the place where Aegeus died. The story goes that he saw the ship returning that had taken his son, Theseus, to Crete, to slay the Minotaur. The ship still sported a black sail; the sailors had forgotten to change it. But Aegeus assumed this signalled that Theseus hadn't survived and, struck by grief, leapt off the cliffs to his death in the sea which came to be named after him.

The cape is a place of atmosphere and magnificence. Chris and John spent the afternoon there, enjoyed a bathe in a lovely rocky little bay and took the bus back along the coast road as the sun was setting.

They did experience one thing that Mike and I avoided in Athens. They suffered an hour's heavy downpour and had to take shelter until it passed. That was probably the only time that it rained during the whole time we were in Greece. They could do nothing but write postcards until it cleared.

Sunium is also a place of tranquility and reflection. I like to think that John took time here considering his vocation. He was often quiet on our holiday and may well have been pondering whether to train for the ministry in the Anglican church. Certainly Chris took an evocative picture of him looking pensive. Within a year, John went on to train at Theological College.

John, pensive, at Cape Sunium and the Aegean Sea

Singing for Our Supper

Friday 21st August

At last we could set off. The black Ford Consul had bench seats front and back, and a gear change on the steering column. This meant we could have three people in the front and three in the back. Even so, it was a squeeze to get all of us into the car in spite of cramming baggage in the boot; we all had rucksacks with us. I remember riding sandwiched in the back with my luggage on my knee. No question of seat belts then for any of us, of course. But as a journey it would be inexpensive. Chris reckoned for the full trip of eight and a half days, it would cost us £6 or £7 each, including petrol.

Mike was the official driver and was registered as such on all the documentation; none of the rest of us had passed the driving test. (In fact I didn't gain a car driver's licence until 1967.) But John had a provisional licence, and in our eyes that was good enough to make him relief driver, if not co-driver. We had less confidence in the car itself as one of my letters home relates:

We're all a bit worried about this car breaking down on us. Although it's a modern one, the previous users, also from our big party, had nothing but trouble. The hooter, the starter, the clutch and the driver's door all went wrong. Still they managed to beat the Greeks down on their price for the hire. That's the general custom which it's taken us some time to get used to.

Our plan was to spend a week doing a clockwise tour of the Peloponnese, that area of Southern Greece like a hand with fingers extended. Mike must have driven us out of the city along the main coast road from Athens to Corinth. At some point, we were glad to stop and have a bathe. This gave us all an opportunity to cool off and clean up thoroughly.

The journey from Athens to Corinth is about fifty miles and involves crossing a narrow neck of land, the Isthmus. By putting the four-mile-long canal through in the late 1800s, the Greek engineers effectively made an island of the Peloponnese, connected to the rest of Greece only by a narrow road bridge. We just clattered over it and didn't stop.

We knew about *Corinth* from classical times and also through St Paul's letters. The apostle had even lived there for two years. But the place itself was a disappointment. Very little remained of interest. We gave a cursory look round, took a few photographs of the ruined Temple of Apollo, looked at the surroundings: a bare mountain with a citadel looming over the desolation.

'Ah, that must be Acro-corinth,' Chris said. This term was new to me and left me puzzling how many other old city states had their own acropolis. I was still feeling pretty subdued since my stomach queasiness lingered. We moved on.

From time to time we caught glimpses of a railway line weaving its way through the countryside and over valleys, heading in the same direction as we were.

'Whole set up looks pretty clapped out.' Mike had his elbow on the door frame of the driver's window. 'I think we've done the right thing.'

★ ★ ★

We had all the time in the world, but we wanted to see so many places: we headed for the very ancient site of *Mycenae* – an early Greek Bronze Age fortress excavated by Heinrich Schliemann in the 1870s. He was an enthusiastic amateur archaeologist and had an obsession with Homer. He believed *The Iliad* in particular portrayed actual historical events and places. Schliemann had worked for several years with blundering energy to excavate what he believed was Homer's Troy. He even adorned his young Greek wife in ancient jewellery he'd found there, and photographed her wearing it. Later, he felt the urge to work at Mycenae. In the shaft graves, he discovered many gold artefacts adorning the remains, including several flattened gold face masks. With typical enthusiastic hyperbole, he announced to the world: 'I have gazed on the face of Agamemnon.' He was convinced he was right: Homer said Agamemnon was king of Mycenae. And so…

In reality, we know now the dates of the masks and the Trojan War don't coincide. The masks are older.

Our party knew what to expect when we reached the barren rocky site: a huge megalithic gateway – The Lion Gate – the main entrance and most famous part of the ancient fortress. We'd often seen pictures of it. Great blocks of stone – Cyclopean masonry – surrounded the site, as if the mythical giants had built the place. This entrance, it seemed, was the most impressive part.

Inside, any gold or magic had long gone. But again we were able to wander at will without paying an entrance fee or being watched by suspicious officials. We knew about one other part we needed to see. It had been dubbed the Treasury of Atreus but was actually an elaborate domed burial chamber often known as a beehive tomb.

We wandered through the arched doorway and into the semi-darkness to look around. No sign of treasure here: only the dome rising above us into stony gloom. The dust floor and a faint, indefinable smell of damp suggested the place might have been used more recently for other purposes.

Late morning now, the sun high in the sky and a great hot stillness beginning to settle over the landscape. The only sound on the air, the itching of the cicadas; the predominant smell that waft of pine brought out by the heat.

Should we go on to Tiryns, the sister fortress to Mycenae, in order to cover both ancient sites thoroughly? We decided to give it a miss and headed back to Argos – a city known even in classical times. Time for lunch.

Great heat often reduces the appetite, but we seemed to retain much of our Englishness and made a point of having something for lunch each day. Melon was on sale everywhere, even at the roadside. We became such experts on the different types, often eating it every day, that I've now acquired something of an antipathy towards it. We always saved our main meal for the evening. One good feed a day. But at lunch time we ate fruit and bread, possibly took a salt tablet or two and had something to drink, water or lemonade – hardly, I think now, a diet to soothe my recalcitrant stomach. But I wasn't the only one: three of us had experienced what we called 'gut rot'.

We knew we wanted to see the great theatre at Epidaurus, but the journey there wasn't straightforward. Argos is at the head of one huge inlet – the Argolic Gulf – and Epidaurus was close to the coast on the other side, looking back across the Saronic Gulf towards Athens. It'd be a cross-country drive, and we needed to get to Nauplion, as we called it, as a jumping off point.

Exactly where we stayed that night is now lost, but our evening meal remains particularly memorable, not for the food, but for the after-dinner entertainment. We were away from the sophistication of Athens now, and the locals were much less used to tourists. As I described it in a letter home:

The Greeks are very curious and will often stand round and stare for no real purpose or reason. We gathered quite a crowd at a café when we flogged their jukebox, and they just wouldn't let us go.

We were sitting outside at a long table with bench seats and, in turn, each of us must have stood up, put small change in the local jukebox, took pot luck on the music and sampled some of the Greek records. The locals were amazed that we enjoyed their popular culture and wouldn't let us leave. Being good hosts must have been important. From somewhere they produced cherry brandy, possibly homemade, and plied us with that. And then coffee. We felt more than welcome.

'This is getting embarrassing,' John said. 'How are we going to get away? I'm ready for my kip.' He stifled a yawn.

We tried to stand up to leave; the men wouldn't let us go.

'No, no, you stay. Drink more wine.' The situation wasn't menacing; we were surrounded by warmth and laughter. It seemed they were keen to sample some of our English culture. But what could we sing that we all knew? We suddenly felt the dearth of popular English traditions.

'I know,' Valerie said, 'what if we all stand up and sing…' The rest of her plan was whispered.

One by one we freed ourselves from the benches and stood up. The Greeks watched, fascinated: we were clearly about to perform something. The letter home says it for us:

In the end we all solemnly held hands and with faces as straight as possible sang, Auld Lang Syne. Amidst applause, we fled with shouts of 'goodbye'.

The Greeks loved our incongruous folk music and accepted it as our farewell performance. We slipped away into the night.

And so to sleep – the first time we'd bed down with Valerie and Ann.

We hardly knew them, they were not undergraduates and were probably already earning, but they seemed happy enough to rough it and sleep on the ground as we did. But equally, for protection, they didn't want to be too far away from us. We outnumbered females at Cambridge eight to one, and college rules then made it an offence to have a woman overnight in your room. In the colleges, sexes were strictly segregated. None of us really knew the etiquette of sleeping with women. But here, with naïve tactlessness, I thought it worth recording.

The other chaps were already in their sleeping bags. But I prepared my flash gun and flared blue light into the darkness. The girls had followed our advice and scattered ant powder in a magic ring to keep any creepy marauders away.

What to do about toilet facilities was a problem for the morning.

Finding a Pit in the Orchestra

Saturday 22nd August
We called it *Epidaurus,* following the Classical tradition we'd learned at school and college. In modern Greek the *u* is also pronounced as a *v* – Epidavros. We were going to see one of the wonders of the Ancient Greek world: a magnificent theatre, a hundred miles away from the glories of Athens. But there would have been no theatre at all if the area had not been sacred to Asclepius, son of Apollo, and god of medicine and healing. The place was the centre of the cult of the god. It's said that patients coming to find a cure slept in the temple of Asclepius overnight and either woke up cured or learned what to do in their dreams. A snake was a symbol of the god since by sloughing its skin it appeared to rejuvenate itself. Sacred serpents were kept in the temples and people believed the ailing were cured by their lick. One ancient author referred to the harmless yellow snakes kept at Epidaurus, some of which are said to be found still in the area. Harmless or not, I shuddered at the thought of snakes slithering over me in the night.

In effect, then, the first hospitals were temples sacred to Asclepius, and Epidaurus was a famous centre of medicine. How much of this we knew in 1959, I don't know. Certainly in ancient times, money collected from grateful patients brought prosperity in the fourth century B.C which meant a sacred theatre could be built.

However, we'd had trouble with the car starter and were delayed before we could drive the fifteen or so miles across country to Epidaurus. There we were really out in the sticks. We parked the car in the heat of late morning, and headed for the theatre, completely ignoring the ruins of the temple of healing.

We wandered onto the site of the huge auditorium which is capable of seating about 14,000 spectators. It opened before us like a huge stone embrace – completely overwhelming. We knew it to be the best preserved Greek theatre of all and famous for its magnificent acoustics. The first thirty-four rows of seats made of local limestone blocks were built into a hillside sometime in the fourth century BC,

Rod of Asclepius (see also Royal Army Medical Corps)

and a further twenty-one rows were added later by the Romans. This vast arena was like an upturned bowl or a modern loudspeaker. We wandered into its open side and found ourselves looking up at tiers of empty seats.

Dwarfed by the size of the place, we felt compelled to test its acoustics from the centre of the orchestra. Rumour has it that you can hear a match being struck or a coin dropped by someone in the centre. Chris stood and recited some lines quietly; later the two girls enjoyed presenting a scene while some of us panted up to the very top in order to take photographs and signal that we could hear every word. To think that they built this place without any sort of roof and it had survived the elements for so long! At that time, access was completely free: we ambled in and were just six of probably less than a dozen who wandered the site.

In ancient Greek times, Epidaurus was an important centre and a thriving community; Homer mentions it. Modern Epidavros has grown important again and flourishes, knowing well how to cater for tourists who seek sea, health spas – and the theatre. We couldn't know that Ancient Greek plays would be regularly performed here – even Shakespeare in English. But in our time the place slumbered, unaware of its treasure, a site only for scholars who passed on, almost by word-of-mouth, the value in visiting the place. And so we, a car-load of youngsters, blundered in, expecting the hospitality and welcome we'd known in Athens. We assumed as a matter of course that the locals would try to rook us and think that travellers could always afford a lot.

That evening we bundled in to what we thought would be a restaurant and found ourselves shown to a table, lit only by a roaring hurricane lamp as darkness encroached. Greek hospitality took over. The lady gave us what she had, I think now, and proposed to charge us five drachmas each (1/3d) for what was obviously a one-egg omelette. Outside Athens many goods had no fixed price, and we always expected the seller to charge what they thought we could afford. Immediately, this price started us grumbling. But we were hungry and needed food.

That table became our base for the evening. I began a letter home by the light of the hurricane lamp, trying to recount some of our adventures in detail. Several times I brushed away moths and other insects that fluttered in. I drained a small Greek coffee.

Thick brown sludge at the bottom of the cup, a few coffee grains lingering on my tongue. Disgusting stuff. No Nescafé out here.

'We've got to beat her down, can't let the bloody woman think she can get away with that.' Mike was back on his hobby horse.

John, always eager to press on, got to his feet and said: 'Shall we wander?' He stood away from the table, the light flashing on his glasses, his knees knobbling beneath his shorts.

I hastily brought my letter to an interim conclusion while the others continued to haggle over the price of what we'd had. The next day I reported the result in my letter:

Yes, they did try to charge us exorbitantly. We managed to knock three shillings and sixpence off the bill, but that was still too much.

I think now suspicion led us to behave badly, not fully understanding the social situation of our host. We paid eighteen drachmas less than she asked for. Drachmas were important to us as well, and the woman had to be content with what we gave her. But what did she think of our manners?

We decided we'd sleep in the theatre that night. Why not? It was open; wandering in was easy. Something to tell our grandchildren about. But as we settled down and I blew up my lilo, we felt a strange foreboding. We were at the interface between our time and the fourth century BC. That feeling of apprehension didn't last. As we prepared to sleep in that vast arena, a bright moon sailed up above the topmost row of seats to the east and spread silver light over the humps of our bodies. I didn't sleep well. I lay close to the centre of the orchestra and every time I turned over on the lilo, the slight movement on the sand sent a crackling echo around the steep auditorium. At one point, I woke up startled and found a dog – also sacred to Asclepius – standing over me and sniffing at me as if he wondered what I was doing there. With difficulty, and as quietly as I could, I managed to persuade him to go away and we slept on until morning.

At least it wasn't a snake.

★ ★ ★

Sunday 23rd August

We woke early and got up at 6 AM. The theatre had been built so that it would be lit by the rising sun and already bright light shone in our eyes. We scattered briefly and made perfunctory ablutions. A cursory glance at the ruins of the temple and other buildings, then off. We crammed back into the car, anxious to return to something resembling civilization. Without breakfast of any sort, we bashed through to *Navplion* and found somewhere as a base. I continued writing last night's letter:

'I'm now sitting on the stony beach at Navplion on the top right hand corner of Southern Greece. Don't expect me to be brown. I've been sunburned twice already and peeled for it. It just doesn't seem worth the bother. Chris has just commented I look very white on the legs considering I got them sunburnt. Whatever makes you think I'm growing a beard? I'm afraid you'll be disappointed. It isn't long before we come home (11 days!) and I think I shall be ready for a bit of Western comfort again...'

In fact I *was* growing a beard which I rarely caught sight of, since we didn't carry mirrors; it had long passed the initial itchy stage: all I knew was that it wasn't as full and Lawrentian as I would have liked. Just disappointing whiskery growth. I'd also taken to wearing long trousers, the khaki drills from Cambridge, as a way of giving my legs some protection.

Sunday morning and everywhere nestling in a religious stillness. We'd had difficulty getting bread for breakfast on Delos a week earlier. But we managed to obtain some boiled eggs and cheese in Navplion to last us for breakfast and lunch. Valerie and Ann agreed to stay on the beach and mind our kit. More inclined to holidaying than resolute sight-seeing, they planned to have a swim and idle the morning away.

We looked up at the towering fortress of Palamedia, as we called it, which loomed above us and jutted out into the bay. There were said to be eight hundred and fifty seven steps to climb, and it would take at least twenty five minutes. Other stories said there were a thousand steps to its highest point – the citadel. I crammed my straw hat on my head, hung my camera round my neck, and we set off, just because the challenge was there. We tramped and panted our way up to an extraordinary fortress built by the Venetians in the early 1700s. Its walls rambled over the cliff edges and commanded a splendid view of the Gulf of Argos.

'I wonder what that place is.' Chris pointed at a small island which sat squarely some distance out in the bay of Navplion.

'Prison probably,' I said, 'you know, like Alcatraz.'

In fact it was the Bourtzi fortress, located in the middle of the harbour of Navplion and once used as military defence. The Venetians completed its fortification in 1473 to protect the city from pirates and invaders from the sea. When we saw it, it had actually become a hotel. But it certainly caught the eye and the imagination.

We spent some time wandering the ramparts, taking in the views. But eventually there was nothing for it but to take photographs and descend the hill again to sea level and our reality.

'Amazing place,' Mike said. 'Extraordinary views.'

We clustered briefly on the beach and looked around for somewhere we could escape the glare of the day and have lunch.

'What about there?' I pointed to an area of the beach, shaded by an awning of bamboo strips.

'That'll be lovely,' Ann said. 'Let's start moving our stuff and bag a spot underneath.'

I blinked at the bright glitter off the water. Still not wearing sun glasses, I lived in the dappled shade the hat cast across my face.

After lunch the urge to start travelling again overtook us all. Enough of Navplion, press on! After consulting the map, we decided we wanted to reach *Sparta,* about sixty miles further south. What we hadn't bargained for was the state of the road. As I put it in a postcard home the following day:

We've been over some pretty high mountains on the way down here. The main road develops into nothing more than a rock-ridden cart track.

After experiencing the fenlands of Cambridge, we found the drive through the mountains of the Peloponnnese fascinatingly scary. We took time to admire the scenery and take photographs.

Greece in summer is unrelentingly dry. All colour is bleached from the landscape apart from the grey of olive trees and the dark green of cypress and other conifers. Grass is brittle and yellow-brown, the earth barren and unforgiving. Grey, bare mountains dotted with scrub loom over the mottled plains. Yet the cicadas love the land and chirp their way through the heat of the afternoon. You cannot see them, only hear their relentless scraping. The day stands still in the heat.

Culture in Sparta

Eventually we arrived at Sparta, glad to reach somewhere we'd heard of, glad, too, that the car hadn't broken down on that perilous drive over the mountains.

'Time for a blow-out, lads,' John said, '-and lasses. I've starved for the last three days.'

'I agree,' Chris said, 'we've lived very cheaply so far.'

The fare that evening was far from spartan. We enjoyed a huge meal of chicken.

We rarely had much to do in the evenings apart from have our main meal, wind down with a cheap brandy or, if we could afford it, a Nescafé. Sometimes we finished an opened bottle of wine before making our way to a place to sleep. We had neither the money nor the inclination to go to any bars or night clubs.

However, in Sparta, not known in ancient times for anything cultural, we discovered something to do that evening. A film was to be shown in the open-air cinema. Perhaps we saw posters advertising it; maybe the waiter where we ate our evening meal enthused about it. Certainly we knew nothing then of what has since become a five-star cult film. They were showing *The Vikings,* a new film, made in 1958, which featured Kirk Douglas and Tony Curtis. For once we were more in the know than the rest of the audience: they showed the film in English, with Greek subtitles. To us after evenings in the Cambridge Arts cinema, watching Ingmar Bergman films, it seemed hilarious hokum. With all the pseudo-sophistication and irony we could muster, we laughed our way through the film which either John or Mike quickly re-christened *The Hairies*. At one particularly tense stand-off between the protagonists, which the subtitles struggled to convey, we burst out laughing, only to find that several of the audience turned round in indignant bewilderment to see what we found so funny.

But my abiding memory of that white-walled rectangular arena with shallow concrete tiers sloping down towards the screen is of the air caressingly warm, the chatter of the projector behind us in that auditorium open to the darkening sky, a place crowded with Greeks who took the film very seriously – and the strong ammonia smell of male urine which wafted out from behind a cubby-holed brick wall to our left and assaulted the senses of all who sat in the seats at the back.

We shared our bed with a river that night. We straggled down to the wide, shallow stretches of the Eurotas, close to the town; there we settled in the middle of the dry river, watched over by reeds, spearing up from little dry islands, or tufts of grass barely clinging to life. We never stayed awake long: the fresh air and the heat was always tiring. Perhaps one of us shifted position, disturbed by a sharp stone beneath or a dip in the river bed which didn't fit his body. I lay on my back marvelling at the misty pinpricks of light above us in the night sky, then turned over. We'd be back in our English life in less than a fortnight, but for now we were hemmed in by silence and the vastness of the Greek sky.

★ ★ ★

Monday 24th August

'You must get to see *Mistras* while you're down there,' someone had said.

I certainly didn't know what to expect and was none the wiser when I learned it was an ancient Byzantine city, abandoned since the 1830s. I struggled with the historical and cultural significance of that civilisation and certainly didn't want to give thought to more knowledge which was outside the canon of our classical education. Cultural fatigue obviously lurked. We even argued how to pronounce the term: some were in favour of 'bizzantine'; others preferred the more ponderous and serious-sounding By-zan-tine. I just about knew it was connected with the civilisation which developed in late Roman times and spread from Constantinople.

We needed to look for a ghost town about three miles away from Sparta. It wasn't on the map since it hadn't yet become a full tourist attraction. We had to rely on word of mouth to find our way and looked out for tiny signposts in sun-bleached wood at certain junctions on the road. For us the journey was a hot and wearisome push to find the place; now the modern traveller can reach there after twenty minutes' drive from Sparta. Mistra is back on the map.

I was in a cultural grump that morning, not really willing to open up to the ruined splendour that lay in front of us. I was hot, I was tired, but even so I took more photographs there than I did in many places. Chris described the place in a letter home as 'fabulous' and 'terrific'. It was certainly very different from any *classical* site we'd visited.

The whole location was huge and set into the slopes and wooded hills of Mount Taygetus.

We left the car about halfway up the hillside and wandered into this strange abandoned world. Our first glimpse of Mistras was of an old building in a reasonable state of repair:

the monastery of Pantanassa. At the time we didn't know what it was called. There were no notices, no plan of the abandoned city. Only later did our classical Greek help us to understand that this monastery was dedicated to Mary, Queen of Everything.

The advantage of being independent travellers, and with our own car, was that we never felt under pressure or needed to rush over the sites we visited. We must have split up into twos or threes, sometimes disappeared on our own. At one point we lost Mike completely in Mistras. Probably tucked away in the shade sketching somewhere. We wandered, investigating whatever took our interest. Such places often induced meditation or reflection, particularly in John who often took time considering his calling to the Anglican church.

The secular buildings lower down the mountain slopes had long crumbled away, but the religious buildings had survived, their circular, scalloped roofs of bright pantiles drawing the eye and the camera. We'd seen them everywhere throughout our travels: some Byzantine churches nestled close to the foot of the Acropolis in Athens. We discovered in places the buildings were still occupied and actually caught sight of one monk going among the ruins.

The whole place had an aura of peace and unreality about it as if we had wandered into another world. The main monastery – Pantanassa – was well cared for, clearly inhabited, but also austere, aloof. The doors were closed against us, the outside heat immense.

I don't remember being able to wander into any of the churches and look at the

frescoes as people can now. But even so, the place must have been prepared to cater for tourists. We found a small restaurant and strolled in to laze there. Chris began a letter home and I wrote a postcard:

I'm sitting now at the foot of a huge hill near Sparta which contains the ruins of a Byzantine town. Overhead are clusters of grapes arranged on trellis work and nearby are two lemon trees. I took a photo of a peacock just now wandering quite wild. Our car is literally like an oven. It's perhaps the hottest we've had it in Greece.

Any traveller on the continent now would take the scene I was so keen to describe as a given and hardly bother to comment on it, but we were new to the delights of Southern Europe and found ourselves in a world so different from home that we marvelled like country cousins, seeing it all through the eyes of enthusiastic and curious strangers.

Mistras was an extraordinary site. In the time we spent there, we hardly took in the size or the complexity of the place. We found the upper city, middle city and the lower – all evidence of expansion over the centuries – damaged, confused and untouched. Mistras had to wait another thirty years before the castle/fortress, the ruined palace, the churches and the monasteries became a world heritage site. I suspect that if I were to return now, fifty or more years on, I'd respond to the place with more interest and enthusiasm than my bored and uninformed self showed on that sweltering August day.

We left late in the afternoon having done a thorough exploration of the place. Chris took a marvellous parting photo of the ruins overlooking the plain of Sparta. We'd have to press on now in order to reach *Kalamai (Kalamata)*, our next stopping point.

Night on a Bare Mountain

Mistras was the furthest south that we travelled on the mainland of Greece. Now we needed to head west. We left the plain of Sparta behind and took what we called a *fantastic* mountain road, almost reaching cloud level. It wasn't the quality of the tarmac – far from it. We found it a slow, winding road, the surface often rough and unmade, with a real chance of rocks falling close to the car. Darkness had settled by the time we reached the seaside town, and, as always when we arrived somewhere new, we headed for the most likely space to offer camping facilities – the beach. Fortunately we found a pitch which was soft and sandy, and there we slept.

★ ★ ★

Tuesday 25th August

We called the town by its old name, but it left little impression on us. Now as Kalamata, famous for its brand of olives, it is the second most populated city in the Peloponnese.

'We've got to do something about this car,' John said. 'What do we do if it packs up out in the wild?'

The car had played up quite often, usually refusing to start just when we needed to get on.

'Do you think we're flooding the engine?' someone said who'd heard about such things.

The only thing to do was club together and get it thoroughly examined by a competent mechanic.

Mike and John prepared to take the car for an extensive garage check during the morning.

'Make sure they don't rook you,' Chris said.

'I wonder if anyone speaks English down here,' Valerie said. She and Ann prepared to go off for the morning. Chris and I agreed to linger on the beach and keep an eye on the luggage. I finished off the postcard I'd begun at Mistras and wandered off to buy a stamp and post it. Chris continued his marathon letter.

'You know, we've no idea what's going on in the rest of the world,' I said when I returned. 'Do you get this feeling of being cut off?'

'You have to assume things continue just the same at home,' Chris said. In the distance we could see Mike and John walking back with Valerie and Ann.

'They say there's nothing wrong with the bloody thing,' Mike said through gritted teeth. 'Waste of a whole bloody morning.' He made sure the two girls couldn't hear him swearing.

'Ok,' John said, 'let's get on the road. You take us out of town, Splot, and then I'll take over.'

Mike wriggled into the driver's seat. 'Hell's teeth! Just like an oven.'

'Where next?' Chris said.

'Inland. Megalopolis. About forty miles.' Mike began to ease the car back onto the road out of town. We lapsed into silence.

'We're in Arcadia now,' Chris said when we stopped again. 'Hardly a rural idyll, is it?'

'I'll say! That was a dull drive,' Ann said as we stopped to change drivers just outside *Megalopolis.*

'Anything to see here? I fancy stretching my legs before we press on.' John yawned. He was the tallest of us and no doubt found the car cramping.

'There's a theatre.'

'Shall we go and inspect it, then?'

'Never going to rival Epi– wotsit, is it?' Mike said. We stood at the top looking down at the scrappy remains.

'Oh, but it's rather a pleasant setting,' Ann said. 'I think so, anyway. Nice and open.'

'Shall we wander?' John set off back through the surrounding trees towards the town. '*Megalopolis* is hardly a big place, in spite of its name.'

We filled up water bottles, found a toilet we could use and clambered back into the car.

'All settled?' Mike put the key in the ignition. The car refused to start. 'Oh, blast the thing. Is that twenty drachmas we've wasted?'

'Leave it a bit and then try it,' John said. This solution often miraculously caused car engines to start as if there'd been no problem.

We waited.

A few minutes later the car started.

'Will it be all right now?' I said.

'Cross your fingers!' Chris sat in the front with Mike and John.

We began bouncing along the road to Andritsaina. A boil of dust rose in our wake.

'You're very quiet.' Valerie sitting in the middle at the back of the car turned to me on her left.

I muttered something about being tired and closed my eyes. But I wasn't all right: a dreaded migraine had crept up on me, and I felt far from well. Was it the afternoon's heat, the flash of the sun on house windows, the bumpy road? I couldn't see properly, and I prayed I wouldn't have to ask the driver to stop so I could be sick.

I slept fitfully, conscious of the sticky contact between Valerie's leg and my thigh in that cramped back seat. *Andritsaina* was to be the base and gateway to our planned stop for the night. We couldn't climb up the road to the Temple of Bassae without first going through the village. I gather that some of the older dons at King's had pooh-poohed Norman Routledge's visit the previous year because, like us, he'd gone up by car. True pilgrims to the classical temple went up by donkey.

We stopped for a breather before doing the final stretch. We'd no idea what conditions would be like. What we did know was that the temple – miles away from anywhere – was built by the same architect, Ictinus, who designed the Parthenon, and that the building was just a little younger than its much more famous contemporary. We stopped and looked back at the winding road through Andritsaina.

'How high up is the place, then?' Ann asked.

Chris put his camera away and looked in a small guide book. 'About three thousand seven hundred feet above sea level. Bit higher than Snowdon.'

'Still some way to climb, then,' Mike said. 'Everybody ready?'

We bundled into the car and kept all the windows open in the hope of some through draught.

The road wound on upwards until we came to the place where we'd spend the night: *The Temple of Bassae.*

It had none of the brightness of the Parthenon. They'd built it out of grey limestone, quarried locally. Although its march of Doric columns gave it grandeur, it seemed dwarfed by its mountainous surroundings. We'd come out to a very lonely place.

A glance around showed little vegetation and no houses nearby. The temple had been built on a rocky plateau surrounded by even higher mountains. It'd be like spending the night at Stonehenge, but far more remote and high up.

Isn't there a piece of music called *Night on a Bare Mountain*? I wondered to myself. My eyes felt heavy, and my head still ached.

'Pretty cut off up here,' Valerie said.

Darkness began to seep around us. We'd decided it best to sleep inside the building. The outside terrain was rocky and might easily harbour noxious creatures. Ants we could deal with, but a snake or a scorpion… Besides, we'd taken a fancy to sleeping in ancient buildings.

'Once daylight goes,' John said, 'we won't be able to see a thing. Only what light comes from the sky.'

'Should still be a moon, though,' Chris said.

I blew up my lilo and nestled it close to one of the inner walls of the temple, as if creating a bedroom outdoors. One by one we finished our food and prepared for bed. Still mid-evening, but darkness and silence settled everywhere. We talked in whispers.

'Spooky this place, isn't it?' Valerie said. 'But I'm not ready for sleep just yet.'

'All right, then,' Chris said, 'Let's tell some ghost stories…'

'I'll just shut my eyes, folks.' John snuggled deeper into his sleeping bag and yawned.

'*…he could sense the ice-chill hand stroking his face,*' Mike's voice was a solemn murmur, '*felt the fingers move round, seize his throat and begin to tighten their grip.* He paused. *The next morning, when his companions woke, they saw him stretched out, staring at the sky, an empty black gauntlet lying on the ground beside his body.*'

'I think that's enough. We'd better go to sleep now.' Ann sounded rather anxious. 'It'll be a long day tomorrow.'

★ ★ ★

Wednesday 26th August

We woke to the jankle of small bells. Hidden by the temple walls, we couldn't see the herd of sheep or goats that wandered the rocky scrub around our sleeping place. The flock must have gathered over night. None of them came into the temple. From some distance away, a shepherd whistled several times and the flock responded by clanking and ambling away towards him. Early morning and very cold. Although the sky was clear and bright, we were thoroughly chilled. The height of our location robbed the early sun of any warmth.

'Have they gone?' John said. 'I'll just go and find…'

We agreed with the girls that we'd make use of what cover there was in one direction for our early toilet, and they'd go off in another.

Mike began singing quietly:

> *Oh, the monks of St Bernards,*
> *St Bernards, St Bernards,*
> *They never get much fun at all.*
> *They rise up right early,*
> *Right early, right early,*
> *And – sniff – through the hole in the wall.*
> *Green grass is yellow,*
> *Green grass is yellow,*
> *Green grass is yellow, is yellow,*
> *And so is the hole in the wall.*

I grinned feebly. My head still ached from the migraine, and it hurt to bend down. This was one of Mike's signature tunes. Very appropriate for this place.

'So who's this temple dedicated to?' He stretched and surveyed the terrain.

'Apollo,' I said, 'Apollo Epikourios. That means *helper*.' I began rolling my sleeping bag up and pulled the air bungs out of the lilo. It always took time to expire before I could fold and roll it to go at the top of my rucksack.

In his mammoth letter home, Chris mentions that there were tourists looking round when we woke up. For me the place was utterly lonely and desolate apart from the distant shepherd and his flock. It's interesting now to see how two of us, both present and both recording our impressions within a day or so of the event, have already come up with different versions. So much for primary sources and historical accuracy!

We breakfasted and had a leisurely morning at the temple. There was plenty to do: wander round the area, looking for the best place to sketch or photograph it, generally imbibe the atmosphere, count the number of columns. I guess we knew it'd have to be a special expedition to bring us back to this remote place in the future, and we wanted to make the most of it.

Nowadays we've taken to calling the place by its modern Greek name: the Temple of Vassae, and the place has also become a World Heritage Site – definitely

Mike's sketch of part of the temple after clambering up onto the walls

part of the tourist trail. But our experience is caught in time. And just in time, too. Now the building is covered by a huge tent, and has been since 1987; the interior glows golden because of the sunlight through the canvas. The grey austerity and majesty we knew has been hidden. People complain now of the long journey up to the site, and the sense of anticlimax in finding it protected, its columns supported by scaffolding to help withstand earthquakes. Why does Apollo the Helper need all this assistance when the temple withstood two millennia of weather, erosion and all that Zeus threw at it?

Time to move off. We began to pack up, tightening the straps on the pockets of our rucksacks. Just a short haul back to the car and then the winding track down to Andritsaina. We'd have lunch there.

'What shall we do with this?' John held up the remains of a loaf of bread, now as hard as the surrounding terrain. 'I don't want it.'

'Sling it,' Chris said.

'What, like this?' John tossed the bread up in a gentle lob and it landed out of sight on top of one of the columns. 'Leave it for the birds. Perhaps an eagle will get it. Yo-ee, yo-ee, yo-ee.' John often used this mirthless laugh to respond to something he found humorous.

But they felt guilty afterwards; Chris still talks about it as if they'd desecrated the site and insulted the god.

We'd heard about a museum in Andritsaina which we assumed contained artefacts discovered at Bassae; we decided to visit it before lunch. But the paucity of display and the poor explanations soon brought out our mockery. John's stomach knew quickly it was time to move on and we headed for somewhere to eat.

While we'd been on the tour of the Peloponnese, we'd contributed to a communal kitty. It'd been easier and one of us had acted as paymaster on our behalf. The fund paid for petrol and all our meals together, but we did have to keep topping it up. Now we'd started watching our own funds, worried we might run out of money before we got back to England. We carried travellers' cheques but could only manage to cash them in big towns or in Athens itself. Most of them had now gone.

'Would anyone mind,' John sounded hesitant, 'if we break off using the kitty now and each pay his own way?'

We all agreed this was acceptable, and after Kitty had paid for our lunch, the surplus cash was divided amongst us.

'Hang on a minute,' Chris said as a trickle of drachmas dropped into his hand. 'I want to see if this shop stocks anything like notepaper. Shan't be long.' He went off and returned carrying a notepad with flimsy lined paper. 'This'll have to do. Don't suppose anyone thinks of writing much around here.'

We began loading the car, postponing for as long as possible the moment when we had to put flesh against the scalding seats.

'Where to now?' I said.

'Looking at the map,' John said, 'we have to head out towards the coast again and then up towards Pyrgos. And then on from there.'

'And where do we hope to be tonight?' Ann said.

'All being well, Olympia.'

We set off on what proved to be the last of the bad roads. Our drives were always leisurely, and we often stopped to admire a view or stretch our legs. On one of our stops, not necessarily that afternoon, we wandered around admiring a ravine and a picturesque bridge which in the heat of that summer spanned no more than a dried-up river bed.

It's impossible to say now where on our travels we came across that bridge. Perhaps it has also now vanished from the land as well as our memories.

From Pyrgos to Olympia we travelled on tarmac road again. 'Thank God for that,' Mike said. 'Those mountain roads must have played havoc with the springs.'

We settled back and relaxed, at last enjoying the smoothness of the fifteen mile ride. *Olympia*, like Delphi, was one of the major religious centres of Ancient Greece and the birthplace of the original Olympic Games. As Classicists, we had to see it. We'd give the site full attention in the morning.

That evening, apparently, we encountered a poet-shopkeeper who impressed us enough for me to consider giving him a mention in my notes. My guess now is he took to boasting of his poetic prowess in the way only Greeks can, hoping to astound the foreign boys who gangled, curious, around his shop while he packed up groceries for us.

We ate a leisurely meal, pleased also to have found a lavatory we could all use. Chris rounded off his mammoth letter of fourteen sides, some on the flimsy new notepaper, and others wrote the last of their postcards. Still more than a week to go, but there was always a risk of us arriving back in England before our own cards. We'd long determined that the best way of communicating with home was to send post via air mail.

We stumbled away into the night, anxious to find somewhere to bed down. Only after we'd settled did we hear the bray of a nearby donkey and pick up the faint zoo smell wafting our way. As I drifted off, I became aware of a persistent dog which barked the night away and disturbed our sleep.

I Feel Let Down

Thursday 27th August
In the morning, I discovered just how rough a night it had been. As I woke, I became conscious of a persistent pain somewhere on my right side. I soon worked out I was now lying on the ground, a piece of rock poking into me. Something had punctured my lilo, and it had let me down. I was cross. Apart from our nights in the Athens hotel, it had given me a comfortable night's sleep for more than a month and had travelled everywhere with me. I debated whether to get rid of it since it was useless and just something else to carry. But I took it home, patched it up with a puncture repair kit and it served me again, mostly for play on the beach or in the garden.

We haggled over breakfast that morning at some small café. Convinced that we'd been served watered-down milk, we managed to get the price reduced. The meal was basic enough anyway: just bread, milk and a little butter and honey. Before we started exploring the archaeological site of *Olympia*, several of us went to seek out the local post office to send our final letters and cards home.

'You'll never believe it,' Mike said. 'They're actually mending the road back there. Didn't think they did that sort of thing in this country.'

I didn't take any photographs at Olympia. For me it was one of the most disappointing classical sites we'd visited. A contemporary souvenir book gives a flavour of the disillusionment I felt:

So little is left standing in the overgrown field of ruins at Olympia that it looks very much like an ancient and peaceful graveyard. Until the year 1875, the whole of Olympia lay buried under the sand and gravel of the River Kladeus. It was excavated by German architects and archaeologists such as Curtius and Dörpfeld. Today the pine trees rustle as of yore in the divine peace which reconciled the warring Greek states during the Olympic Games.

I was convinced now that I liked temples, theatres and other Classical buildings in sufficient state of repair or survival that you could at least appreciate what they were once like. So Cnossos, Epidaurus, even Bassae had done it for me. But here the tumble

of stones and pillars did little more than depress. In places, even now, sixty years on, the impression of dereliction remains.

But modern Olympia has been tidied up and laid out like an archaeological park with gravel paths and better signs describing the ruins. A lot of money has been spent, particularly on the museum. When we visited, Olympia still slumbered, unkempt and abandoned, crying out for a sympathetic eye to present it to the world in an intelligible and accessible way.

Chris, however, found majesty in its ruined splendor, even though the traces of the Ionic column he photographed had been set up only to give an impression of how it might once have been.

Apart from being buried under 16 feet of yellow silt – the sand and gravel of local rivers – the area was also subject to earthquakes which had done much to topple and scatter the columns of the temples and other buildings.

This place, once so important in ancient times, epitomised the irony of Shelley's line in *Ozymandias*:

Look on my works, ye Mighty, and despair!
Nothing beside remains. Round the decay
Of that colossal wreck…

Here once stood one of the Seven Wonders of the Ancient World – the giant statue of Zeus; at least two mighty temples had dominated the scene as well as places for wrestling, horse-racing and other sports. Olympia was never a city-state like Athens or Sparta, or even Corinth or Mycenae. Like Delphi, it was more of a sacred area, but when we saw it, hardly well-defined. To use modern parlance, we wandered around the original Olympic village which had grown in size over nearly four centuries, had been excavated in the late nineteenth century and then, so it seemed, left to nature. In reality the Germans did more excavation work in time for the Berlin Olympics of 1936, and later the workshop of the great sculptor Phidias was discovered in the 1950s, shortly before we visited. I think it unlikely we were even aware that Phidias had created the massive statue of Zeus for Olympia there, in that very place.

We dreamed our way round that vast site, not knowing where we were or what we saw. Chris managed to take a picture of John resting by what is probably the temple of Hera, Queen of the Gods. But we had the place to ourselves: no one to educate us, no one to disturb us. I wonder if we ever managed to find the arched approach to the stadium which was the central area for the ancient games.

Even now the stadium is hardly prepossessing, but it is used regularly by modern visitors trying the challenge of running races there.

Apart from Athens, Olympia is the only Classical site I've revisited since our trip to Greece. It, too, unsurprisingly, has been declared a World Heritage Site, and as such is much better presented and laid out. A lot of money has been spent making it more visitor-friendly. The modern museum is magnificent and welcoming.

One great treasure links our visit there and modern times. It was the prize exhibit of the old museum; it is even better displayed now: *The Hermes* of the sculptor, Praxiteles.

They dug out the statue from the shale surrounding Olympia, reassembled it and presented its marble beauty and magnificence to the world. It remains close to the place where it was found and has never been hi-jacked by Athens or – heaven forbid – by the British or any German Museum.

It is sad that our last visit to a truly Classical site had been such a disappointment. Now, I say, Olympia is worth seeing again. Now you can revel in the vastness of the site, the better layout and the marvellous sense of space.

But it is the Hermes, holding the infant Dionysus, that was the highlight of our visit then and remains so now. It is truly a κτῆμα ἐς ἀεί – a possession for all time (Thucydides 1.22)

The stadium at Olympia.

The entrance to the modern museum, Olympia.

We began to think of moving on and left Hermes in his curtained seclusion in the museum, surrounded by a bed of sand in case another earthquake should topple him. I was lucky: I never had to do any driving and was able to snatch a quick sleep in the car. Wherever we sat, though, the car was cramped and hot. I was often in the back. That day we made do with a cheap lunch somewhere and began the long drive to *Patras,* a town on the western end of the Gulf of Corinth. It's now the third largest conurbation in Greece, and an important port. Though we stayed the night there, we found it uninteresting and didn't bother to explore much. It was Thursday evening; we weren't due back in Athens until Saturday morning. But already dwindling cash reserves and the end of the holiday cast a shadow over us.

Throughout our time in Greece, Mike seemed to hate having his photograph taken, and whenever we posed as a group, usually for Chris, Mike would self-consciously take up a funny stance. I'm glad though that somewhere on our trip round the Peloponnese, Chris did decide to take a memento picture – one for the road.

We slept again in a dry river bed that night under the shelter of some olive trees. 'This is as good as the Ritz,' someone said. 'We'll sleep all right here.' It was already pitch dark.

'Just a minute,' I said, 'I want to take a picture.'

'I'm going to sleep,' Valerie said. 'I'm tired.' She snuggled down in her sleeping bag.

I prepared my camera and the flash: Chris lay on his back, still as a pharaoh's mummy. And Mike…

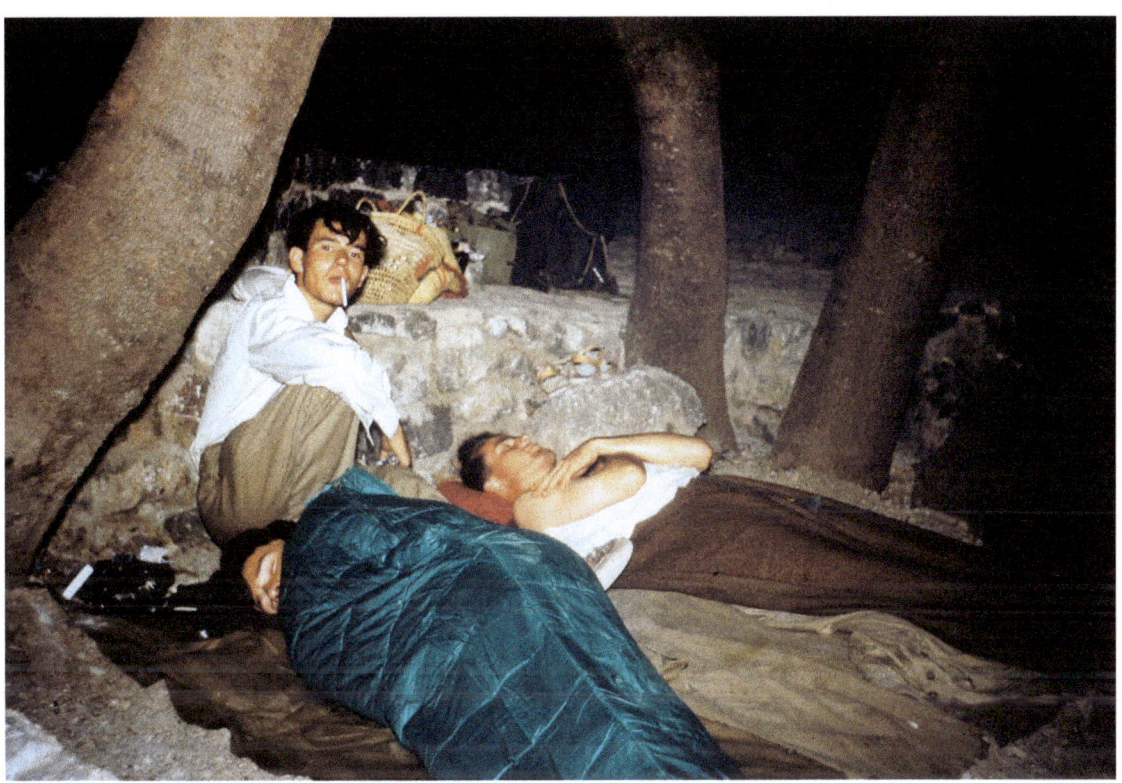

Friday 28th August

We all woke to the blear of morning, disturbed by the sounds of chatter and laughter. Someone nearby had already started work. We heard the clop of donkeys' hooves on the hard ground, the creak and strain of wicker baskets.

'They're going grape picking,' I said.

John eased up from his pit, and we four wandered over to see them at work.

'Yia sou.' Chris smiled.

'Yia sas,' said an old woman. 'Kali mera, ti kanete?'

We all smiled broadly and felt awkward. Kali mera – that meant *good morning* but…

'Americani?' One of the men looked us up and down.

'No.' We all shook our heads, but kept smiling. 'What's the word for no?' Mike hissed out of the side of his mouth.

'Tsermani?' The man narrowed his eyes.

'Ohi,' Chris said, 'Angliki.'

Relief and good humour spread over the pickers' faces. Handshakes all round, both parties shuffling in pleased embarrassment. Nothing more could be said between us but we'd made firm friends for a brief moment.

'Well, they were jolly coves,' John said as we wandered back, each carrying a large bunch of grapes they'd given us. Fortunately we did remember the Greek for thank you.

'Want some grapes?' Mike called to the two girls who were now ready for the day. He held out his bunch to Valerie. 'There's plenty.' He turned quietly to me and muttered: 'How are your guts now? Can you cope with fresh fruit again?'

'Should be OK,' I said.

'We're going to find the beach,' Ann said. 'Have a dip and freshen up.'

'Mind if we join you?' Chris said. Having been inland and away from any water except the odd tap, the four of us hadn't had any sort of bathe for a week, and we'd do well to wash the dust and sweat of travel off before moving on again.

Breakfast turned out to be very poor that morning, no more than boiled eggs and sugar. Were we economising, or had we found another place where supplies were low?

'I think he's saying no,' John said. 'Oshi,' the waiter said and again tipped his head up as if about to nod. He rolled his eyes upwards at the same time.

'Awkward bloody language,' Mike rumbled.

Later, when the waiter had gone, we tried practising the alien gesture until it felt as if it belonged to us.

We had twenty-four hours and only about 130 miles to go before we had to return the car. Even if we averaged 40 mph it'd take about four hours. So we could afford to be leisurely. In any case, we always took driving in Greece very cautiously for fear of the impulsiveness of Greek drivers. What's more, in the event of any accident, chances were that we'd be blamed as being young, inexperienced and unused to driving on the 'other' side of the road.

So we could consider this day an opportunity for relaxation rather than sight-seeing. The main road back to Athens ran along the edge of the Gulf of Corinth. The sea was blue, untroubled and very inviting. We bathed three times that day. What did it matter if we had to struggle back into wet costumes each time? They soon dried in the sun. On one occasion we pulled off the narrow road and parked on the scrubby verge. Below us the sea, and a wide, stony beach. Other bathers were already there, but the place looked too appealing to ignore.

We writhed into our costumes, using the car or towels wrapped around us as our changing room. We strolled down and enjoyed the sun and the largely empty beach.

Never one for lazing in my swimming trunks and chary of the hot sun ever since Mykonos, I wandered around, my camera round my neck, looking for a suitable photograph. The others lolled and relaxed, feeling the sun beat on their shoulders.

Chris looked up and spotted me standing silhouetted against the sky: 'Good child-bearing hips, Richard!'

I said nothing. Gave a sickly smile, probably. I'd always been self-conscious about my broad pelvis in proportion to the rest of my skinny frame, and now with me just in swimming trunks, he'd spotted it. Damn!

Strange remark to make, though; I've never forgotten it.

Lunch-time crept towards us. 'It's no good,' John said, 'have to feed my face. I'm starving.' We made a break from the usual fruit and bread and found a little café which served us spaghetti. This was a novelty for us – equally strange, foreign food. It was only two years after the BBC's April Fool's Day spoof, narrated in all solemnity by Richard Dimbleby, about harvesting spaghetti from trees in Switzerland. Spaghetti wasn't widely-eaten in the UK and considered by many an exotic delicacy. But to us that day, the pasta was very welcome as a stomach filler.

Off again towards Athens, taking our time, enjoying the scenery. We were crawling through the village of Xylo Castro – now a pleasant town and sea-side resort.

'Sleepy sort of place,' Valerie said. 'Must be siesta time.'

'I bet that horse finds it hard work, pulling that cart.' I pointed to a nag lumbering out of a side road towards us.

'Poor thing, in all this heat,' Ann said. Her voice rose sharply. 'Look out. It's not going to stop.'

John jammed his foot on the brake and we screeched to a standstill. Still the horse came on and bumped into the front wing of our car.

'Idiot!' Mike shouted out of the nearside window. The man on the cart merely waited a second then steered round us and let the horse plod on across the road.

'I hope it wasn't hurt,' Ann said.

'What about the car?' Chris and Mike both jumped out. 'Fortunately not,' Mike said as he inspected his side of the car. 'No dents or scratches.' He glared at the retreating cart. 'Idiot!' He did the obscene Greek flinging gesture with his hand. This *Moutza*, as it is called, is the equivalent of giving someone the finger – a definite insult.

'Mike, don't!' I shouted. 'Get in. We don't want trouble.'

'All OK, boys and girls?' John started the engine again and we began to move off.

Late afternoon we came up to the Corinth Ship canal. We'd now completed our circular tour of the Peloponnese and rejoined the road we'd taken out of Athens.

'Mind if we stop?' Chris said. 'I want to see if I can get a picture from the bridge.' We parked somewhere safe and Chris strolled back to get his picture. The canal looked so narrow, certainly not wide enough for two ships to pass.

'Must be a one-way system,' John said. 'How long is it?'

'About four miles, I think.' Chris adjusted the focus on his camera.

'You wouldn't want to fall in,' I said to Valerie. 'You'd never get out.'

Somewhere before we reached the small town of *Megara*, the road was straight but rather narrow; it was already early evening, the air hot and still, and we were cruising along calmly. John was driving. Approaching us in the opposite direction was a big lorry and, as always, we slowed down and eased over to our side of the road even more.

I Feel Let Down

'This idiot's cutting it fine.' John could see in his mirror another car approaching us rapidly from behind. 'He hasn't got room.'

The car tried to overtake and began to edge us over.

'He's running us off the road,' Chris shouted. We all sat tense, expectant.

The driver didn't collide with us but swerved in at the last minute and the rear wing of his car managed to lock onto our front bumper. Now the two cars were effectively one unit. The speed of the other vehicle dragged us along for about forty yards before both cars stopped half off the road.

We sat in shocked silence.

'Get out!' Mike hissed his instruction to John. 'Get out now!' He'd been sitting relaxed and bare-chested – off duty. But now he got out of the other door and raced round the back of the car and stood on the driver's side in front of John. Appearances at this moment were important. It had to look as though Mike was driving, not John.

The driver of the other car – an archetypal Greek in short-sleeved white shirt and dark glasses – got out of his car, looking shaken and scared. He must have known it was his fault.

Ann began to take the number of the car and asked him to print his name for us in English letters.

'Use your camera,' I said to Chris. 'Take some pictures. Evidence…'

Chris began focusing his camera and took three photographs of the scene. Both John and Mike looked shaken and uncertain. John rested his arm on the roof of the car, hoping, no doubt, that he wouldn't have to lie about who was driving.

When the Greek discovered we couldn't speak his language, he became more cocky. A big grin spread over his face. A local field-worker appeared and the Greek driver called him over and tried to bully him into being a witness in his favour – without much luck, fortunately. We took the driver's name, and the number of the car and any other particulars we could think of.

In return he asked for Mike's licence, studied it closely and dismissively pointed out Mike's date of birth – 1938 – as if the accident must have been caused by him as a mere hare-brained youngster.

We were all subdued and shaken up, some of us no doubt wondering how we'd explain the damage when we got to return the car.

With a little jolting and bouncing, we managed to get the two cars unlocked from each other. Luckily, all we'd got from the incident was a bent bumper.

'Let him go,' Valerie said. 'Let him get right away from us. I'll be glad to see the back of him.'

'We were lucky not to turn over.' Chris wriggled back into the car.

We sat in glum silence and watched the Greek drive off.

'I don't believe it,' Mike said. 'He's at it again!'

A hundred yards down the road, the Greek driver did exactly the same manoeuvre: with another vehicle coming in the opposite direction, he cut in sharply in front of another car going in his direction.

'Maniac, absolute bloody maniac!' Mike immediately apologized for swearing in front of the two girls.

'Who's going to drive?' John said in a quiet voice. He still looked shaken.

'It's got to be you, Bayley,' Chris said. 'Even if it's only a few miles. Find your confidence again. Wasn't your fault. Climb back in the saddle, and all that.'

We eased back on the road and continued our journey, our last day with the car now thoroughly spoiled.

Chris sat looking through the scribbled details of the other driver. 'You're not going to believe this,' he said. 'You'll never guess what his job is. It says here 'Αστυνομία (Astynomia). Our road hog is a policeman.'

Name That Tune

Saturday 29th August

We drove into Athens in the early morning for breakfast. This was all carefully planned; by staying out of the city for one more night, we'd saved ourselves the cost of the hotel. Besides, we weren't expected. We camped for the last time somewhere near *Daphni* – the ancient monastery we'd first seen three weeks earlier, on our way to Delphi.

We all drove to Cooks in Constitution Square to return the car and put our case concerning the accident damage. 8.30 in the morning: still we worried about being rooked, especially as funds were now so low. But the people at Cooks couldn't have been more friendly and helpful, and we immediately felt reassured. A man from the car hire company appeared and we again explained our story. Nevertheless, the deal was that we had to pay for the damage – some 300 drachmas (about £4, Chris reckoned), and the firm undertook to prosecute the speeding policeman on our behalf, and then refund us the money, if the case was successful.

'I've got photographs of what happened,' Chris said, 'which I can get developed.' He was confident they'd show our tyre marks in the dust of the verge, where we'd been dragged.

'Yes, you must do that,' the man said. 'You send me photos. When you leave Athens?'

We told him and he assured us there'd be no difficulty in winning our case. He even gave us a written statement that they'd prosecute the other driver and give us our money back. Chris said he'd be able to pick up the photographs on Monday evening, and he'd take them into Cooks the next day. Then began the process of hunting through our pockets and wallets, or borrowing from someone else. We managed to stump up the total required – fifty drachmas each. Reassured, we left Cooks, parting on very good terms.

'That's encouraging, lads,' John said as we walked away. 'Nice man.'

'I'm pleased they knocked some money off the bill because of the starter and the faulty speedometer,' I said.

'Yes, ninety-six drachmas, that's OK. I reckon that's about twenty-three shillings,' Chris said.

We were, of course, *born yesterday* and never heard any more about the matter. From this perspective, it now seems obvious that having received money for the slight damage, the firm wouldn't go to the expense of any prosecution.

Pity the young Englishmen abroad and far from home.

We made arrangements to meet the girls for an evening meal, said a brief farewell and headed back as a foursome to our base: the Lux hotel. Valerie and Ann went back to the YWCA.

After the early-morning excitement, we drifted into a lazy day. I sat on my bed, leaning against the wall and wrote two letters – the last I'd send from our Greek Odyssey. No guarantee they'd reach home before we did.

One of the features of the holiday was a sound: pop music. It seemed to have followed us everywhere on the mainland. We first heard it when we camped on the beach at Edem, close to the night club. There, it was played over and over again, wailing and echoing into the night so that we thought we'd never sleep. As far as I was concerned, it was typically Greek, the bouzouki music so prominent and recognisable. At the time, I considered Athens as the frontier between East and West – where Europe stopped and Asia began, a position more readily accorded now to Istanbul – and what fascinated me was the mixture of the two cultures which seemed to meet in this one pop song. The modulating wail of some of the singing seemed to me to carry the flavour of India and all the mysteries of the Orient. What determined me to try and buy the record was that it had disturbed our peace again only the previous night when we camped near Daphni. It'd make an ideal souvenir. But I had only one problem: I didn't know what it was called, or who was singing it, only that it was current and very popular, judging by the number of times it had assaulted our ears and shattered our sleep.

It was getting near the mad-dog time of day when we should have been indoors, but Mike and I set off and found two or three record shops and asked them if they could identify it. I became quite adept at explaining the bouzouki element of the music and even tried to sing it to the shopkeepers who were only too keen to help. But the real difficulty was that the tune was acutely un-hummable to someone trained in western harmonies. The shopkeepers couldn't recognise what I was trying to sing, and nor, if I was honest, could I. Our encounters broke down into giggles and polite laughter from the Greeks. Smiles all round. They tried playing record after record in the hope that we would land on the song.

'No.' I shook my head. 'It's not that.'

In the end, out of embarrassment rather than anything, and conscious that they wanted to close the shop for the afternoon break, we gave up and left empty-handed.

'Can't be that difficult,' I said, 'it's so popular.'

I, at least, took a siesta that afternoon – something that touring the Peloponnese had prevented. There, we just had to keep going whatever the heat.

We met the girls in the early evening, as the air cooled and the shadows grew longer, and went to the *Ideal* restaurant, a place we'd come to love and frequent – somewhere which served good food at reasonable prices. It was also a way of saying goodbye to Valerie and Ann since our agreement to go around together ended when we returned the car. I don't remember seeing them again after that, though they must have travelled back on the same train.

We set off for an after-dinner stroll, and I determined I'd buy a book of souvenir photographs of Greece. I'd worked out that many of my photo-slides would be unusable because I'd stupidly forgotten to reset the lens aperture after a low-light shot and many of them would be horribly over-exposed. We came across a typical kiosk, somewhere on America Street, close to Syntagma Square.

There I bought *This is Greece – The Mainland* – a photo book, costing 7/6d in our money – 37 drachmas. I was really pleased with it and have kept it and referred to it ever since.

'Some of these magazines are a bit near the knuckle,' John said. 'Look at that! Seems like pornography to me.' He became convinced in later years that the Lux Hotel where we stayed was actually a brothel – which is why accommodation there was so cheap.

We shook our heads and muttered something about the looser morality of these continental countries. We soon saw dirty significance in the word Ζαχαρο (Zacharo) which I was convinced had some sexual link with sugar and all sort of sweet delights. We wandered back to the hotel, laughing at this new side of Athens we'd discovered, quite convinced that we knew what we'd find if only we dared to push open the doors of the Φρολιξ (Frolics) Bar.

★ ★ ★

Sunday 30th August

My notes say we had breakfast at dawn today. Incredible. But there was already a sense of pressure, a feeling we must do a variety of things before we left Athens. Who knew when we'd be back, if ever? We began to go off in pairs or even mooch around on our own.

This left Mike and me very much to our own devices that morning. We decided we wouldn't leave Athens and wandered around looking at things we hadn't taken in before. The ceremony of the Changing of the Guard in front of the Tomb of the Unknown Soldier still takes place every hour, on the hour, with a major changeover at 11 AM. The Evzones – guards dressed in traditional costume with flowing tunics, skirts and pom-poms on their feet – paraded in almost comical slow motion, high-kicking their feet as they marched and occasionally striking the pavement with their boots.

Almost like fancy dress, I thought.

'Not English, are they?' Mike said with irony, no doubt thinking of our busbied scarlet soldiers on duty in London.

We wandered on from Syntagma Square until we came to the Byzantine Museum.

'Give it a go?' Mike asked.

I've more memories of us sitting outside in the gardens and putting the world to

rights and philosophizing as he and I so often did, rather than being stunned by any of the exhibits. We were back in the early Christian world again with frescoes, and soulful, serious-looking images of Christ or the saints. Bored and on overload, I gave the exhibits a cursory glance. For my taste, a culture too far.

Another siesta that afternoon. It was so useful to have the room in the Lux hotel as base. I did snooze on the bed, but Chris worked on completing his last letter home. Timing was all important. We'd discovered letters took about two or three days to reach England if sent by air mail. But we'd got used to postcards taking at least nine days. The longest postal delay was when we sent something from Phaestos itself on Crete. It only proved how cut off the place was.

We'd all agreed to take advantage of the free entry to the Acropolis – a feature then of Sundays and Thursdays in Athens. Chris was keen to go up at sunset when the colours of the marble were wonderful and the shadows much better for photography. So that was the main target for the day – that, and another visit to the theatre of Herodes Atticus, this time to see an Ancient Greek comedy – *The Birds* by Aristophanes.

But we spent the late afternoon strolling round parts of Athens we hadn't bothered with much before. We wandered south east from Syntagma Square through the tree-lined National Park towards the Olympic Stadium. I'm sure I had little idea then of its significance or history. It was reconstructed and developed on the site of an ancient stadium for the celebration of the first of the Modern Olympic Games in 1896. It just seemed a rather dull open ellipse with seats for spectators, an obvious evolution from the one at Olympia itself.

All the time we were drifting towards the Acropolis but approaching from a direction we'd not used before. We stopped to stare at Hadrian's Arch, strangely isolated on the edge of a main road.

Shortly afterwards we approached the ancient Theatre of Dionysus, which, from the road, looked intimate and battered in comparison with the grandeur of Epidaurus or Delphi. It had been set into the hillside of the Acropolis and was able eventually to hold 17,000 spectators; certainly the area would have been known to the classical Greek dramatists who featured so strongly in our studies. But this later construction looked diminished. We sat on the marble benches and struggled to imagine any play being performed there. It had, of course, grown and been modified over the centuries.

We had to rush now. We found a taverna, probably on the edge of the 'plaka' (the historical neighbourhood around the northern and eastern slopes of the Acropolis) and had a hurried meal. It would have been a place to linger: part of the building had been carved out of the rock. Dining in caves would have been a novelty. But we still planned that quick dash up to the Acropolis to catch the sunset tinge on the marble.

Back in the Herodes Atticus theatre, I was surprised to see someone I knew. Grant Carson had played the part of The Watchman in the Cambridge Greek Play, *Antigone*, in which I had been the leader of the chorus.

The play had been produced in the Arts Theatre in all the obscurity of the original Greek during the Lent Term of that year (1959). Grant was the sort of chap you looked up to – a jovial hulk of a man, probably older than us, having done his National Service before coming up. Certainly more streetwise, as we might say today. Athens was once again the meeting place of civilization. He was not in our party and must have come to the city privately. I introduced him to the others, but we had to settle quickly and stop our jesting as the performance was about to start.

We were no wiser about this performance than we had been for the *Agamemnon* earlier. There was just more to look at. We didn't know then that we were witnessing a landmark performance of Aristophanes' *The Birds*. Karolos Koun's legendary direction of

John's cartoon imagining me as Leader of the Chorus in Antigone

the play was produced in 1959 as the result of a co-operation between renowned Greek artists of the time in music, visual arts, dance and theatre. Stunning spectacle it may have been, but we still didn't understand much of what was going on; however, the play did give us some idea of the origin of Cloud Cuckoo land – an expression still in vogue today.

After the play we stood around 'yarning', as I called it then. Because we were so far away from home, we knew little of what was going on in the world other than what people told us or we gleaned from letters from home. There'd been a plane crash we didn't know about, and Grant mentioned another cast member from *Antigone* who'd been killed in a car crash in Africa; we also heard there'd been widespread flooding in Austria which caused Valerie's brother to be stranded for some time.

'I hope our train gets through OK,' Chris said, 'and that Salzburg has dried out.'

What really galled, though, was that the weather at home was extremely hot. What was the point of travelling all this way only to find everybody at home would be as brown as we were?

We learned one thing that evening: we should have gone to Zacharo while we were on our Peloponnesian Tour. It wasn't some sleazy joint in Athens after all; it was a small town which has the longest beach in Greece.

'You missed something there,' Grant said. 'Marvellous beach, virtually deserted. Well, I'm off for a little late evening fun.'

'Where are you going,' I said, 'the Frolics Bar?'

'No, no contest. The Rio's the place to be. Beautiful girls. Join me.'

'Bit full of himself, your mate,' Mike muttered in my ear.

We hesitated and looked at each other.

'Not me, lads, I'm for my kip.' John yawned and made a move. And that decided us.

★ ★ ★

Monday 31st August

We were late rising the next day. We started by turning out our pockets and counting the money left in our wallets.

'It's no good. Have to start economizing, lads. Dosh won't last otherwise.'

Most of us agreed with John that cash was tight. But none of us considered cutting out buying presents or souvenirs to take home. The others had a frugal breakfast, probably little more than fresh bread and coffee. I had βουτηρο μελι – the magic mixture of butter, bread and Greek honey which still epitomizes an Athens breakfast for me.

We began to go on separate errands. I returned to see George Douzinas, the Greek who'd befriended me ten days earlier before we went round the Peloponnese. I found his hardware shop, and we spent some time yarning in his office at the back. He spoke English competently and I quickly decided he was a good Greek – someone I could trust. He explained how the villagers we'd encountered away from the capital were primitive and unsophisticated: 'That is why we have Ministry of Tourists.' I smiled discreetly at the thought.

He must have been to England since he spoke knowledgeably and enthusiastically about Cornish women. Hard to say whether he was drawn to Celts as a type; they were clearly different from the Greek girls who so enchanted us.

'If you have geograph map, I show you places I know.' One thing he did promise – which alarmed John when I told the others about it: George invited me to a wine-tasting festival – 'where you drink as much wine as you like!' he said.

'How do you do it, Pike? The queers swarm round you like flies.'

★ ★ ★

I was still determined to find a record of the Greek pop music which had plagued us. I must have got to know a girl who worked in one of the music shops in the city. I knew her as Mary, and if nothing else I decided I'd buy a record from her. We repeated the elaborate ritual I'd developed of trying to sing or hum the tune, such as it was. I was getting desperate now. She didn't recognize the tune I wanted. In the end, I decided to buy a 45 rpm record anyway. It'd be a memento, if not an actual souvenir, of that damned tune.

'Ok,' I said, 'I'll take that one.' I hesitated, disappointed. 'Could I just hear the other side?'

Mary turned the record over and began playing it. Within seconds, and certainly after the first wail of singing, I shouted, 'That's it.' I felt a huge grin spread over my face. 'That's the tune I'm looking for.'

'Ah, yes, Mantoumpala.' Mary smiled at her success.

She slipped the HMV disc into a plain cardboard sleeve ready for me to take away. I felt thoroughly elated that I'd finally tracked the tune down and couldn't wait to tell the others. I have the record still.

There is a sequel to this story. It's possible even now to listen to the tune in the version we heard more than fifty years ago. If you Google *'Mantoumpala'*, in that Greek spelling, the music comes up, and you can hear Stelios Kazantzidis singing our song. For a few minutes, you too will be lurched back to a time when four young men lay in their sleeping bags on a sandy beach close to Athens, and desperately tried to block the sound out.

My instinct at the time was right: the song does have connections with the East; Kazantzidis was very impressed by an Indian actress he saw in films and wanted to celebrate her in song. Further exploration online will reveal the Greek words and their meaning. How strange that we were pop-pickers all those years ago. The tune's now regarded as a Greek classic.

I hurried back through the heat of midday Athens to join the others for lunch and tell of my success. We ate cheaply as our budget dictated, saving our hunger for an evening meal. After that, we split up. I was quite happy to indulge my siesta habit and snooze away the heat of the day; the others decided they'd make one last trip up Mount Lycabettus.

After my nap, I wandered the streets on my own, window-shopping, perhaps, or watching people. At some point we all met up again. Chris now had the prints of the incident with the car, and it was important to take them quickly to Cooks and show someone our evidence.

'Ah, yes, very good, thank you very much.' The man took our copies, tucked them formally in an envelope and put them away.

We never heard anything further about the incident.

We'd still time to kill before we could allow ourselves an evening meal. We began desultory exploration of the streets of Athens. We set up a plan to wander round the roads behind Constitution Square, where Cooks was, taking a right-angle turn whenever we came to a junction. At one point, we came across our companions from the train compartment, Merle and Janet.

'How are you getting on?' Mike said.

They gave a wan smile. 'We're incredibly broke-'

'-and hungry,' Janet added.

I'd like to think we invited them to join us for an evening meal at the *Ideal* restaurant that night, but it seems not. Either chivalry had died, or they insisted they could manage.

The *Ideal* had become a place where we felt comfortable. We often went there, particularly as we knew what the prices would be. The restaurant served very good food, often in large portions, and for us was an excellent way of ending our day. Just as it became a fixture in our last few days in Athens, so we were delighted that one of the waiters, Χρηστος (Chrestus) had begun to recognise us now. So far away from England, the *Ideal* brought a flavour of home, a place where we'd be welcomed.

I'm happy to say the place still exists in Athens, still in business after opening some ninety years ago. But Cooks has long gone from the nearby square as, no doubt, has the idea of *Poste Restante*.

★ ★ ★

Tuesday September 1ˢᵗ

Our departure loomed. We were looking forward to getting home but the prospect of the interminable train journey appalled us.

For me, it was mostly a day of souvenir buying. On Mykonos I'd steadfastly resisted buying the decorative knitted shoulder bags with dangling tassels, and I thought a circlet of worry beads was stupid. But I found it difficult to find suitable things for some people at home. It was a perpetual grumble my mother uttered at Christmas time: 'It's so difficult to know what to get you men.' Her compromise solution seemed always to be socks or handkerchiefs. But it'd be pointless trying to take Greek versions home. Nothing distinctive about Greek socks or handkerchiefs. I spent a great deal of the day window-shopping to no avail.

We all went our separate ways that day. Mike took himself off to Piraeus and then spent the day sketching on the Acropolis. Chris went around taking photos of daily life in Athens, inspired by the souvenir book I'd recently bought. His pictures have proved to be very valuable illustrations of our time there.

After all the stomach upsets we'd experienced, we'd made our diet practically fruitless now. We'd eaten so much melon over our time in Greece that it had begun to have a stomach-turning effect whenever we contemplated it. What I did long for in Athens, as the call of home grew stronger, was apples – crisp, succulent apples with all the sharp taste bred in an English climate.

Back in the hotel, after my siesta, I wrote letters and cards for the last time and prepared them for sending. Since the basin was free, I did the last of my clothes-washing and set items over chairs or the balcony to dry – not difficult in that heat. I looked at my watch: shops would re-open at 5 PM and I'd be able to buy more presents. I made a decision that afternoon: I'd buy only kitsch as souvenirs. I headed for the Acropolis, knowing there'd be stalls along the way crammed with bad-taste goods. Athens was still an intimate city then, and it was no surprise to meet Mike coming back from his sketching. I don't think I'd seen the statue of the Greek Discus thrower in the British Museum, but I certainly knew of it, and for me it epitomised Ancient Greece. That late afternoon, I bought cheap miniatures of Discobolos – the Discus Thrower – and, of course, the Hermes of Praxiteles we'd seen at Olympia. What happened to them later, I have no idea. Like many souvenirs, they were lucky to survive the journey home; they left no trace in my life.

I went my own way that evening. Time for one last adventure. The others, no doubt, went off to the *Ideal* for their meal. I'd saved my hunger up, knowing that George had said he'd take me out for a meal. I'd remembered his promise: 'You drop in here any time you want, and I take you out for very good Greek dinner with Greek wine.' Either that or a wine-tasting festival. I cannot believe it wasn't a definite arrangement; I wouldn't have just appeared, expecting food. Something was set up, but it wasn't what I thought at all.

I went round to No 9 I. Pesmatzoglou, a side street where their hardware shop was situated, near the National Library of Athens. Both George and Ellen were there. Unsurprisingly, there'd be no socialising until they'd closed the shop that evening.

'Ah, Richard, it is your last evening, yes? You cannot come again another day?'

'No, this time tomorrow we shall all be on the train home.'

'Because I am so sorry, I have business appointment tonight. But I will see you later when I return.'

The arrangements appeared to be that George and Ellen would go home, and I should take a trolley bus to Patissia (one of the city's northern suburbs). I was given precise instructions how to find their house: I would be entertained there.

And so I was. But even now I cannot work out what was going on that evening, and what was expected of me. Was I an innocent abroad? I certainly didn't have a proper meal that night.

I managed the transport without difficulty and found the house. No sign of George all evening. Ellen, as I always knew her, was a few years older than me – say twenty-eight, and one piece of information I'd gleaned about her was that she was single and had a baby. British reserve kicked in, and I nodded inwardly to myself: *Understood. Of course.* Ellen was not stunningly attractive: she had the Greek black hair, naturally, but her face was already muddied by early aging. I spent the whole evening with her, most of it alone. She entertained me first on the porch of the house and later in the living room, which was lit only by a single table lamp. It seemed everything was set for intimacy. I was introduced briefly to her mother who didn't speak English. A pantomime of nods and smiles between us, then Mother withdrew discreetly and left us to it.

But to what? Night had fallen, the house was dark, and we spent two or three hours together. The only food I had was loukoumia and water, and I suspect that with my hunger I wolfed the lot.

What was going on? At the time I suspected I was being groomed as a possible husband and father for Ellen's baby. I did learn she was a divorcée. I guessed that divorce in a religious country like Greece was frowned upon. To find a new husband quickly was an ideal solution. I trust I behaved impeccably. But what sort of marriage catch was a scruffy, bearded student in crumpled clothes?

Ellen spoke English quite well, and we spent the whole evening in semi-darkness chatting. But what we talked about was interesting. At the time, we seemed to have discussed British men of letters. But is it just coincidence that characters like Maugham and Wilde came up? My notes give only a hint, but I must have told her about my encounter with Angelo. Was she trying to find out whether I was gay or not? Did she expect me, a red-blooded male, to make a move on her and compromise myself? We talked of Shakespeare about whom I knew little at the time; she took me up onto the rooftop where the night air hung heavy with jasmine. Was this a scene stage-managed for romance? All the time she seemed to be probing, trying to find out whether I was suitable marriage material. The conversation seemed light-hearted on her part, but still I detected an underlying tone of seriousness.

What I chiefly remember about that evening was the atmosphere. The conversations have faded, but I can still feel the intimate tension between us in that darkened room. We sat about two feet apart, and there was on the air an unspoken expectation of –

something. Had we just run out of conversation, or did she expect me to kiss her? Did she want me to?

I didn't. Nothing happened. When it became obvious that George was not going to appear after all, I made my excuses and left.

It was very late when I returned to the hotel; Chris and Mike were already in bed and asleep. I crept into that hot room and slipped wearily between my sheets without disturbing the others.

I never saw Ellen again. I did call in the shop to see George briefly the next day, but his sister wasn't there. Pity, I would have liked to see her in the light of day to see whether my fears or assumptions were confirmed. But I certainly felt I'd made a friend in George and wanted the following Christmas to recognize that. Trained well, no doubt, by my mother, I gathered a selection of typical English things and sent them out in a parcel to Athens. I even included a present for the baby. I had no thank you in response. I probably continued contact on a few more occasions, but, as I remember it, heard nothing.

I was in Athens again at Christmas 1976 and curiosity led me back to that same Athens street. The shop was still there, George still the proprietor, now probably nudging fifty. He was polite enough and claimed to remember me, but I don't think he did. I asked after Ellen but I learned she'd moved away. Those encounters seventeen years previously meant less to him than they did to me. Perhaps honey-tongued promises were all I could really expect of Greek hospitality, however friendly and welcoming he seemed at the time.

★ ★ ★

Wednesday 2nd September

There's nothing more tiring than hanging about on the day of one's departure. Our train was not due to leave until 8 PM. We had the whole day to fill before we could get under way for home. All of us viewed the train journey with dread.

In one of my last cards back to England I wrote:

I shall be sorry to leave Athens – I like it best of all I've seen in Greece.

In another, I expressed my apprehension:

The train journey is going to be hell, even more so than it was coming here because there's nothing to look forward to, and we shall be itching to get home.

I even asked my folks to cater for 'a five week thirst for tea.'

I spent the day in dilatory shopping, mostly hunting for suitable souvenirs. I remember buying a jar of the dark, liquid Hymettus honey which I loved and which encapsulated the Athens breakfasts for me. That was for an uncle and aunt. Months later I discovered their tastes did not coincide with my own. The jar remained on their shelf unopened. You cannot put Greece in a jar and bottle it.

Inevitably, I bought some *loukoumia*, knowing that the delicate fragrance and taste would evoke expressions of delight at such an un-English delicacy. On one of the many stalls full of mock ancient souvenirs, I was intrigued to find a miniature model in hardened rubber or plastic of an ancient Greek hoplite – a heavily armed soldier, complete with helmet, shield and spear. In my first school, a year or so later, I took him into the classroom for the children to examine and was upset when he was returned to me, after his journey round the class, disarmed and damaged. Schoolchildren are natural vandals.

My notes say with typical hyperbole that I was concerned that day to 'buy souvenirs by the dozen'. What else I bought has long gone into the dustbin of time – except one thing. In spite of my own antipathy to the fruit after five weeks of eating it, I took home a melon. I knew my parents would enjoy such a rare delicacy. It certainly fared better as a hump in my rucksack than the banana had done on the outward journey.

Around 4 PM, I paid that visit to George Douzinas for the last time. He apologised for his absence the previous evening, apparently out doing some business with a Frenchman. He made excuses for Ellen's absence from the shop, saying she was tired. I left, wondering if I'd out-stayed my welcome the previous night.

We'd decided to leave any food-buying until 5 PM; that way we wouldn't have to carry it around all day. For the last time, we visited the fruit market and stocked up on provisions for the journey. There was one other souvenir I'd have loved to bring back. In that late afternoon heat, the jasmine was smelling particularly fragrant, but there was no way a spray of that would survive three days of rough handling.

We allowed ourselves two treats that early evening. The first was one last meal at the *Ideal*. That made sense. That'd keep us going until morning when we'd be out of Greece.

'What a pity,' John said. 'Our waiter isn't here tonight.'

'Please say good bye to Chrestus for us,' Chris said.

The waiters came out onto the pavement to say farewell. Handshakes all round. They assured us they'd pass on our good wishes to the one who'd become our friend. Outside on the street, we had our second treat: a taxi to the station, all four of us and our bulging rucksacks.

'Taxi!' I called to Mike.

'Where to, mate?' We'd gone into a Goon Show routine.

'Drive me up the wall!'

'Right, mate!' He growled at the back of his throat in best Ray Ellington manner.

We arrived at the station in good time for a 7 PM assembling and were back in the care of Commander Soulsby once more. This time, however, we weren't so lucky. The Greek authorities hadn't booked seats for our party. Right through to Ostend, it was going to be a case of making do and finding space where we could.

The train pulled away punctually and we all felt the pangs of regret at our departure. We'd been in Greece a long time. As the train gradually picked up speed through the northern suburbs, we had a glimpse of a sight we'd come to love. Nothing else mattered: one last view of the Acropolis up on its hill – and we were whisked away into the gathering darkness.

Goodbye Athens, goodbye Greece.

Homeward Bound

That night I really learned about roughing it. We had no reserved seats, and no chance of sleeping as a group in a compartment as we had on the way out. We were lucky we could leave our luggage in the racks. There were always other people struggling to gain a seat in our compartment. It became increasingly obvious we'd have to sleep in the corridor. Or stay awake.

'They do say it's possible to sleep standing up,' Mike said.

Someone came out with the expression, 'sleeping on a clothes line' – a reality of the doss house in poorer times.

We did try something like it, jutting out our elbows and resting our heads on our hands on the shoulder-height rail that ran along the windows of the corridor. I certainly became very drowsy and may even have nodded off. But in the end I came to a desperate decision. I'd sleep on the floor, come what may. My last night in Greece was spent huddled in my sleeping bag against the side of the compartment which was nominally ours. I became inured to the kicks of passers-by. At one point someone even spilled water on me.

★ ★ ★

Thursday 3rd September/ Friday 4th September
The next two days passed in a blur of discomfort. My notes say we saw Mount Olympus from the train – the highest mountain peak in Greece and famed as the home of the gods. How we managed that I don't know: it's 270 miles from Athens, and, even at Greek-train-trundling speed, we must have passed in the dark at about 1 AM.

We were beset by crowds at Thessalonica, sixty miles later, and people shouted and bundled onto the train, and began hunting for seats. New arrivals are rarely considerate towards existing passengers. I gave up all attempts to sleep on the corridor floor at this time. Two hours later we reached the Greek border at Idomeni and soon left the warmth and ease of Greece.

We began the long, slow haul through Jugoslavia, but fortunately everything did seem quicker, the bureaucracy less officious, the gradients smaller, and the journey passing more rapidly. We again had a splendid meal in the Jugoslav restaurant car. We'd kept back *dinars* for just this moment; we didn't care about those in our party who'd had to convert their money to *drachmas* in order to stay solvent in Athens. One advantage of eating at a table on trains is that you're comfortable, have a good view, and it's an extremely pleasant way of passing the time.

When we got back to our compartment, our places had been taken. An old Slav sat nodding quietly and staring defiance at anyone who might want to shift him. Another place was taken by a woman who nursed a fretful child on her lap. The child's noisy grizzling was very wearing on those who'd had so little sleep. Nothing for it but to stand and sway bleary-eyed in the crowded corridor. This time I had no Tatiana to beguile me with her eyes and seductive talk.

In Belgrade, mass panic broke out again as people wanted to get off the train while new passengers were determined to cram on board. Again, we adopted the shift system in the hope of protecting some space for ourselves; again when the train lurched on its way, we tried sleeping on our feet in the corridor. There were now several babies in our compartment; the mothers took our proffered places as their right and gave no thanks, or even smiles. So much for British courtesy. Our eyes ached. After two hours, we did manage to claim our places in the compartment, but received envious stares from other travellers in the corridor.

Various characters slipped into and out of our travelling life: there was a slimy, fat Greek whom I thought worthy of note and our hatred; a chaplain appeared in our compartment, and I was surprised when John, already tired, rounded on him as the man tried to get us to give up our seats: 'Why don't you push off?'

We could have been refugees. We had little status, even though we were travelling the whole distance to Ostend. Everyone was out to protect his own interests; aggression lurked and humanity was lost. The journey was proving to be worse than we could have imagined. There came times when we had to leave our seats: to go to the toilet or to refill our water bottles if the train stopped long enough in a station.

People shouted insults at us in Austria which only served to steel our resolve; we wouldn't budge. One woman went so far as to try to force herself into a place among us. *A bit orf*, we thought.

Only when we reached Salzburg and had a twenty-five minute stop did we feel in touch with civilisation again. We stepped down from the train and bought some chocolate and re-filled our water bottles. We poured away the two-day-old water which was warm and tasted sour. No doubt we washed ourselves and also made use of the station toilets.

At this point, we decided to abandon any hope of claiming seats in our allocated coach and managed to find a spacious Austrian carriage The metal boards slotted onto the outside panels indicated that it was going all the way to Ostend. If we could only get in this coach, we'd be in comfort.

'Is it all right?' I asked a train attendant. 'Do you have room?'

'O, ja, you're welcome.' The man gave an expansive gesture.

We climbed on board , found an empty compartment with no reservations and took possession. With luck, this'd be our home for the next fourteen hours. Ostend was still 1000 km away.

A little while later the attendant slid back the compartment door. 'You boys want eat? You can have food in *Speisewagen…*' he hesitated.

'Dining car,' Chris said.

'Yes. I ring you up when is time to eat.'

'That should be interesting,' Mike said. 'How'll he do that?'

A short while later, the steward came down the corridor tinkling a tiny tea-service bell. 'Ok. You come now.'

We still had a few German Marks left so we sidled down the corridor to the German restaurant car in expectation of something to rival the Jugoslav food. But meals on trains have never been luxurious and have been the butt of jokes for years. Only recently, travelling first class through Germany, I was regaled with tough slices of ham, a soupy sauce, mashed potato and – sauerkraut. Adequate, but hardly *haute cuisine*. But we were travelling student class then and certainly felt we had a poor meal that evening.

'I tell you what, lads, I'm going to nick a few sugar lumps,' John said. 'Keep us going.' We had to feel we'd had our money's worth.

But the meal did one thing for us: it made us tired and after our stressful, sleepless time we'd all bedded down long before we reached Stuttgart.

★ ★ ★

Saturday 5th September

We slept well in that Austrian coach. Even though we were woken at 5.45 at the Belgian border by an official, we managed to go back to sleep and finally surfaced, feeling incredibly relaxed at 7.30. Such late rising was unknown on the train.

We began packing and re-organising our rucksacks, ready long before time to leave the train.

One of us came back from the toilet. 'Everything's clean down there, thanks to Belgian Railways, I suppose. But someone's made a hell of a mess in a compartment two or three doors down. Litter all over the floor.'

'Bloody proles!'

Eventually we pulled into Ostend at the end of one of the longest continuous train journeys available at the time. At its post-war height, the service ran three times a week. During those three days of travelling, we'd crossed out of Greece, chuffed across the many states of Jugoslavia, sped through Austria and Germany and finally traversed Belgium. However, we were already passing into history since the through-journey to Athens was discontinued in the early 1960s. Air travel had begun to take over and the need for long-distance train journeys disappeared. You could travel to Athens by air in roughly three hours rather than the three days it had taken us.

At Ostend, Chris, always keen on his beer, bought some duty-free, hoping for a refreshing drink after our journey. But the regulation was that he mustn't open any until he was safely back through British Customs.

'Damn it, foiled!' he said.

On the boat back across the channel, I found somewhere and slept for an hour and a half; we took our time over a large lunch and saw when we came back on deck, the white cliffs clearly visible. We'd be in Dover within twenty minutes and on time!

'Blimey,' Chris said, 'Don't the colours look dull?' We'd lost the brilliance of the light on the Continent and faced the drab weather of England again. But at least everywhere was green, even at the beginning of autumn.

'Well, lads, I think we can safely say our time in Greece was one of the most remarkable holidays we'll ever have.' John hefted his rucksack up into the luggage rack of our Southern Region train. A mutter of agreement from us all.

The sense of relief and anticlimax when we reached Victoria was almost palpable. London at last. Nothing further to say, nothing more to endure. Too tired to make much of farewells, the others shouldered their rucksacks, we shook hands somewhat awkwardly and they disappeared on their separate ways. We'd all see each other in Cambridge for the new term in a month's time, anyway.

We'd arrived early, our scheduled time being 5 PM. My girlfriend, Meg, was coming up from Edgware to meet me, so I had a three-quarter hour wait. I couldn't set off or we'd miss each other, our paths crossing somewhere in the dark tunnels of the Northern Line. It didn't occur to me to find a public phone box. Probably didn't have the pennies.

While I stood in the wide space of Victoria, my rucksack leaning against my legs, and surrounded by the echoing noise of station business, I had one last noteworthy encounter. My eye caught sight of an attractive dark-haired girl wearing a bright kilt and a red tartan shawl. She may even have worn a beret.

'You're still a long way from home,' I said. 'You won't be going back tonight, will you?'

'Ach, nein, tomorrow I will travel in Scotland. Tonight, here I remain at London.' She looked round for someone to meet her. We talked for some time until her friend arrived.

'Enjoy your stay and *gute reise* tomorrow,' I said.

That was the last of my Wonderland experiences: was she a German Scot or a Scottish German? *Do cats eat bats? Or…*

It was lovely to be greeted by Meg. We embraced warmly, she stroked my beard and laughed. 'Aren't you brown?'

We dived down the rabbit hole of the Tube and passed our journey back to Edgware with much yarning about my experiences, particularly how I'd managed to find *Mantoumpala*.

'You look well,' she said as the tube train burst out of the tunnel into evening sunshine.

'I hope my parents have got the boiler going,' I said. 'I haven't had a hot bath since I left London.'

I stood in our living-room, dishevelled, bearded and weary. My dad, always one for the killer welcome, took one look at me and said: 'You can shave that bloody thing off, for a start.'

It was good to be home to a predictable life again.

Chris, the photographer with five weeks' growth of beard.

Mike tries to impress John with his Goon humour.

Author's Note

John did enter The Church of England and served in a variety of parishes in Lincolnshire, his final post being as a vicar in Lincoln itself, and as a Canon of the Cathedral. He died in 2009; *Chris* had distinguished service in The Bank of England, later with particular financial responsibilities in Japan and the Far East. He retired in 1995; *Mike* became a GP and worked until retirement in practices in Northamptonshire, Hertfordshire, Lichfield and finally Somerset; *Richard* worked in education serving as a teacher, lecturer, administrator and finally as Head of English in a rural Nottinghamshire comprehensive school. He has never retired; he works now at his first love – writing.

Let John have the last word ……

Two cartoons portraying the author, back at college as seen by John.

thys same hystorick pyke was, we are afeared, unsuccessful. It was observed by hys friends that he was never quite the same afterwards — which was a great pity, for he was a promysing ladde.

Acknowledgements

All reasonable attempts have been made to find and attribute authorship of the other photographs in the book. I am most grateful to be able to include them in this book.

P 54   DAPHNI, Christos Pantocrator, (Wikimedia Commons) Source photographer The Yorck Project

P 60   DELPHI, The Oracle of Apollo – picture courtesy of ODYSSEY Adventures in Archaeology (13:10: 2011)

P 70   DELPHI, Auriga Delfi – The Charioteer (Wikipedia) picture taken March 2008 by Raminus Falcon

P 70   DELPHI, Head of Charioteer Photograph taken Feb 2007 by Gunnar Bach Pedersen

P 73   ATHENS, NAMA Poséidon.jpg – National Museum of Athens (Wikimedia)

P 73   ATHENS, Head of a Kouros – National Museum of Athens – photograph taken by Ricardo André Frantz 1 January 2006.

P 74   Dying Trojan – Aphaia pediment warrior W-VII Glyptothek Munich 79.jpg (Wikimedia Commons) Photographer unknown.

P 74   ATHENS Chapel of Saint George, Lycabettus, interior.jpg (Wikimedia Commons) Author – Tomisti 2011

P 86   ATHENS Temple of Hephaestus (South), Athens – 20070711.jpg (Wikimedia Commons) taken on July 11 2007 by the uploader, w:es:Usuario:Barcex

P 115   MYKONOS – Peter the Pelican (Wikimedia Commons) Photograph taken May 2003 by Heiko Gorski

P 162   PELOPONNESE – Image of Isthmus of Corinth courtesy of NASA Earth Observatory, taken on May 9 2005

P 164   PELOPONNESE Treasury Atreus.jpg , Mycenae taken 20 January 2006 by Carlos M Prieto (Wikimedia Commons)

P 167   (PELOPONNESE) Rod of Asclepius original by CatherinMunro

P 168   (PELOPONNESE) Ruins of the Temple of Asclepius the abaton File:20100408 epidaure29.JPG (Wikimedia Commons) taken 8 April 2010 by Jean Hausen

P 172   (PELOPONNESE) The Bourtzi Fortress (Nafplion) taken by User.FocalPoint 26 April 2006

P 182   (PELOPONNESE) Theatre at Megalopolis – Picture featured originally on Chatephuck.wordpress.com Picture taken 16 October 2012. Attempts to trace the original owner of the file or the blog have regretfully proved unsuccessful.

P 209   ATHENS A tram passing Hadrian's Arch in the early 1950s. Author – gichristof (Wikimedia Commons uploaded 26 February 2009)

P 215   Alamy – Stock Photo – Greece Epirus Metsovo Souvenir shop selling woollen bags

P 220   ATHENS The Acropolis as viewed from the Mouseion Hill. (Wikimedia Commons) photo taken by Christophe Meneboeuf 11 June 2011 http:// www. pixinn.net

P 227   The Four Reunited 29 March 2006 Photo by courtesy of King's Parade (A Magazine for members of King's College Cambridge.)

*Mike's sketch of the view
from our window at the Lux Hotel*